R.M. BASTIEN

AN EXECUTIVE GUIDE TO
THE NEW AGE **1**
OF VOLUME ONE | UNDERSTANDING THE GAME
CORPORATE IT

What You Should Know About Corporate IT But Were Never Told

*To my mother, who taught me the
meaning of principles.
To my late father, who showed me how
to speak one's mind.*

TABLE OF CONTENTS

TABLE OF FIGURES

ACKNOWLEDGMENTS

This is my first book. If I had known then what I know now, I'm not sure I would have started this endeavor. I probably would've procrastinated a few more years until retirement. That's why I'm fortunate and forever grateful to those who pushed me into this or helped me when I was sinking in a tar pit. Daniel Fitzpatrick, who regularly and constantly reminded me that I ought to put my ideas on paper. Derek B. Lewis, a business-book missionary, who gave me hope and foundational recommendations. Virna Lucia, for her awakening spiritual guidance during troubled times. My beta readers and field experts, providers of invaluable industry feedback: David Jacques, Alain Lorthios, Patrick Morlon, Michael Simoneau, Gueorgui Hodoulov, Mehdi Merabet and Clovis Brullemans. The editing squad, Julie Fitz-Gerald and Jennifer McClorey. The graphic and layout artist, Victor Taranovici. And my muse, goddess Artemis, sent down from Mount Olympus to lovingly endow me with the energy to plow into this project on nights and weekends.

PREFACE

The realities you are about to discover are largely unknown or misunderstood by non-IT managers and executives. You are often left wondering what's going on behind the opaque, lingo-protected curtain of technological know-how.

That's why I've done everything possible not to pull you down in technical details. I've avoided the mumbo jumbo trap that many IT-cognizant people use to make you think you should trust them blindly. The only things you need to be knowledge-able about in order to get the picture are management basics about people, business, money, incentives, processes, account-ability and quality.

But before you read on, you should be aware of a few important assumptions I made about you and your business, as well as some crucial precisions.

The IT in Question

To ease the reading and deliver on my promise of not getting technical, the idiom "Information Technology," or from now on just "IT," has been stretched more than I'd like. Distinctions could have been made and dependencies outlined between IT and related concepts such as "Information Systems" (IS), or "Digital" this and that.[1]

But nowadays, technologies are pervasive and intermingled with the organizational fiber and its environment. Furthermore, in many organizations, the group of people in charge of all this has been labelled IT for some years now, so that it has become the customary epithet. So I have made the stretch of using only the two letters IT to encompass information technologies, their application to the business you're in and the teams that make this happen.

Infrastructure

Although the word IT will be used to cover everything touching information technologies, a distinction must be made about what is commonly called "IT Infrastructure." This term refers to the servers piled on racks in data centers, the cables running in walls and ceilings, the laptops of your employees and the whole array of standard software that is never developed in your organization, but always purchased.

Many of the issues alleged in Volume 1 are much less severe for the infrastructure portion of IT, as it has matured at a faster pace and benefits from more agreed-upon industry standards, benchmarks and unit cost metrics. Infrastructure is vendor-centric, and this makes a big difference. This book describes known issues that derive from the absence of such benchmarks, standards or metrics and will explain the reasons for their absence in the other areas of corporate IT.

Size Matters

Small businesses do have their issues with information technologies, but they are of a different kind, and readers from smaller organizations might have some difficulty relating to the problems and solutions presented in these volumes. Smaller organizations buy or rent most of the IT assets they need. They generally use third-party providers with turnkey contract engagement models. Compared to medium and large organizations, their IT platforms and teams are proportionally much more externalized. As we will see in more detail in Volume 2, this makes a world of difference.

Same for those organizations that are small because they are young; they just don't have the huge IT estate — or burden — made from years of complexity-generating behavior.

What Is Your Business?

The business you're in is of the utmost importance for the purpose of getting value from this book. I assume that IT is not your core business domain and that you operate in one or more of the various industries, such as transportation, banking, insurance, public-sector services, car making, etc., that *rely* on information technology to support their operations. I assume you're not in an organization that designs, develops *and sells* information-technology products. The fact that one sells the fruit of its IT development in a competitive market makes a palpable difference. If that's your case, then many of the issues presented in this book simply do not apply.

Sources

It is my sincere hope that you will find in this book some gems that will enlighten your understanding of many IT-related issues.

The pictures I've painted are far from being rosy, and you may wonder if your own organization is as bad as those you'll read about. As always, it depends. What I'll describe is based on three decades of working in the trenches, all the while observing, wondering, asking questions, getting some answers or getting none at all. I have personally seen everything described in this book, repeatedly over the years, in all of the organizations I've worked with. My direct experiences have been reinforced and confirmed by readings and by discussions with other IT practitioners in different organizations, industries and geographical locations. Nothing here applies only to one organization or one point in time.

That being said, it may be that your organization does not suffer from some of the illnesses described in Volume 1. In that case, well, it just does not apply in your case. Good for you. But be careful about the source of information that leads you to conclude you shouldn't worry about certain aspects. Maybe you should read on and make up your own mind before positively concluding that it doesn't apply.

Agile, the Overused Word

It has become necessary these days, with the growing adoption of the Agile™ method, to clarify this word. With the exception of the previous sentence, every time you read the word "agile" or "agility," it will refer to the generic definition found in English dictionaries since the 15th century: "Ability to move quickly and easily," applied in our case to an organization. It will never refer to a trademarked development method.

[1] *Oxford Living Dictionaries: American English.*
https://en.oxforddictionaries.com/definition/us/agility. Accessed: February 2018.

This book deals about profound issues that have outlasted decades of technological evolution as well as significant improvements in the way the IT function operates. Agility is the objective, but Agile™ offers no relief to these deep-seated problems.

One Last Disclaimer

This book doesn't contain many sentences in the third-person point of view, but when it's used, the masculine or feminine form of the personal pronoun has been elected randomly.

INTRODUCTION

It was a Friday afternoon and probably the last meeting of the week for all the IT staff, IT senior directors and IT executives in the room. Have you ever noticed how sometimes Friday-afternoon meetings get a bit less focused, less serious or even facetious? I believe it's probably because it's the end of a long week of hard work. On a Friday afternoon, people occasionally say things they wouldn't have said during a Tuesday-morning meeting.

I was presenting a very simple quality-control framework for the architecture and design of IT solutions. The reception was at best lukewarm, albeit polite. Then came a moment I will remember for all my life: one of the executives declared in a confident sigh, "Anyway, we'll get our 55 million next year, just like this year."

She said it. She added the missing fragment of wisdom that allowed me to put all the pieces together at last.

The attendees all smiled or nodded and went off to wrap up Friday and move on to their weekend satisfactions. I was also nodding, but for reasons other than approval: Of course! Why hadn't I seen this before with such clarity? Corporate IT runs a lucrative, very low-risk business, with one, sole captive customer that pays all wages, expenses and bonuses.

It was a comfortable position when I began my career 30 years ago and is still as cushy as ever in today's highly competitive world, where no one is shielded from market disrupters and hungry competitors — no one but your IT staff.

Corporate IT's business success is totally dependent on your own business success. In three decades working in corporate IT, I've seen budgets vary. I've seen waves of layoffs and staff optimizations. I've seen outsourcing, offshoring and nearshoring. But never have I seen IT-budget variations based on pure IT performance.

The fluctuations in IT budgets — and especially IT investments — were always in sync with the corporation's financial health. The company shows profit growth? The IT budget should rise next year. The company made another acquisition to augment its market share? The total IT budget should jump significantly during the IT-merger phase. In the end, corporate IT — and its allotted budget — is either treated like any other support function or blended into business projects that have clear and measured returns on investment. In both cases, the IT function escapes real head-on-the-block evaluation of its performance, at least for all change investments.

The IT executive on that Friday afternoon was right. The organization is heading to profit growth at a steady cruising speed? Then corporate IT can safely bet that its budget will be steady in the foreseeable future.

Your IT team has no competitors and a highly-customized product that no one else can offer. As long as the client is financially healthy and relatively happy about the work being done, this business model is a dream.

What is your IT staff calling you and all of their non-IT colleagues in areas such as marketing, operations, sales, distribution or human resources? They're calling you "the business."

It carries a lot of suggestive weight. It means that the business you're in is a business other than IT. It means that IT's business is IT, not banking, travel, offshore exploration, insurance or whatever your case may be.

If one of your IT staffers loses her job or quits, you can be sure that she'll find another job in IT; the industry in which she'll find it is of lesser importance. If one of your IT employees is asked what business he's in by a stranger at a social event, he'll most likely answer IT-something, not banking, insurance or retail. I've done it my entire career, and I don't recall any fellow geek claiming to be in any business besides information technology.

In other words, IT is running its own little business inside yours. Don't get me wrong: they genuinely love and respect you, along with the business you're in! They love it insomuch as it generates the revenues required to pursue their own careers in the IT field.

Do You Have These Suspicions?

Do you have the everlasting impression that your corporate IT continues to show signs of an immature field, even after decades of experience?

Are you left perplexed when you look at the technological quantum leaps that humanity, including your business, has witnessed over the past decades — and then compare them to their net effect on the efficiency and speed of your corporate IT function?

Do you have the suspicion that behind the curtains of technological know-how lies a monstrous amalgamation of old and new technologies, created by the same corporate IT team that is struggling with it?

Is your mood ranging from remotely curious to downright fed-up with your IT department's inability to keep up with the pace of your business?

Are you coming to the same conclusion as mine: that when it comes to responding to changing business needs, corporate IT has been, at best, steadily mediocre throughout the years?

If you've answered yes to any or all of these questions, then I have two pieces of good news for you.

First, you're not paranoid. After three decades of working in corporate IT, I can assure you that these are items you should be concerned about. All the IT professionals I consulted, before and during the writing of this book, recognized running into these issues again and again in their own, at times painful, real-life experiences.

Second, this book will provide you with a refreshingly different view of where these issues lie. Unfortunately, the paths that have been used so far to deal with them lack a deeper understanding of their non-technological root causes.

This is not about yet another miracle product, vendor, method or technology. You're probably under a deluge or of technobabble sales pitches that imply in some way that big data, disruptive innovation, AI, IoT, machine learning, augmented reality, DevOps, micro-services or the acronym of the year will save you or propel you into another sphere where your current issues won't exist anymore.

We'll take a different approach: we'll aim to understand, in Volume 1, how corporate IT's underperformance in certain crucial areas — such as the quality of what is delivered — is not related to technologies or methods. You'll discover the true culprits: management and governance issues that lead to unwanted behaviors that bog down agility. In Volume 2, you'll grasp that by working on the allocation of responsibilities, the establishment of decision rights and the definition of new, measureable accountabilities, non-IT executives can make a lasting difference. By the end, you'll be equipped to redesign the corporate IT model for good and get to the next phase of maturity.

The Business-Agility Boat Anchor

Business agility is all about reacting faster than your competition to a changing business environment. Or better yet, it's about disrupting the business environment — and your dismayed competitors — by being the first to implement something, from new prices, products or services to profound paradigm shifts in customer experience.

But nowadays, this can't happen without the support of information technologies. They'll be entrenched in your business processes or even serve as the cornerstone upon which your strategies are based.

Any change, whether it be a new application, a new mind-boggling technology or a revamped business process, will always impact many IT components. Upstream, downstream or sideways, there are invariably other applications, systems, databases, interfaces, links with external entities, etc., that need to be taken into account. You can never start from a clean slate.

Even a start-up company, although it has much more leeway, needs to interact with partners, vendors, customers and other stakeholders through existing IT components. That's called "integration."

Simply put, integration means making the new stuff work with the existing stuff. The direct business value of integration work is often marginal. Integration, in the best cases, will be a requirement for the business solution to work. In many other cases, however, it will be a necessary evil, the consequence of an overly complex technological ecosystem. One thing is absolutely certain: the more complex the environment is, the more integration work will be required. After decades of involvement in the design, development and integration of business solutions, it is my belief that this complexity accounts for a significant portion of the total costs of projects.[2] It is nothing less than an anchor that slows down your IT team when it's trying to deliver in a timely manner.

Technology is often complex because that's what it needs to be in order to support highly sophisticated solutions. The end result, however seamless, natural and user-friendly it might be, often hides a wealth of interacting components, each one masking other technical ingenuities. But that's not the type of complexity I'm referring to. As you'll come to understand in this first volume, your IT portfolio is plagued with unwanted complexity.

This state of the environment is aggravated by the way corporate IT deals with the problem. In project-oriented IT[3], project managers consider the state of the existing IT assets as input parameters, in other words, as givens that need to be taken

---

[2] My personal observations suggest that integration costs range from 25 to 40 percent of the total cost of the IT portion of business change projects. Researchers and industry observers [7] come to similar figures.

[3] We shall get deeper into this topic in Chapter 5.

into account in the project-planning process. They don't need to have an opinion on these assets and often may not have the skills to measure their qualities anyway.

Allow me to draw a parallel. In a bridge-building project, the geological configuration of the landscape on the two sides of the river to be crossed is taken as a given that will be considered when the solution is engineered and the schedule and cost are estimated.

The fact that sand will require more consolidation infrastructure than granite is just a parameter and is taken as it stands. No one will question why in heaven there is so much sand right where we need to build a bridge!

In a corporate IT project, the state of the assets that need to be dealt with is also taken as a given, as if God had created them a billion years ago. This is obviously not the case, nor is it a project management oversight: a project is, by definition, a temporary endeavor with a beginning and an end. It is normal practice not to question the assets in place and to just make sure that risks are identified. What happened before a project's start and what happens after its closure is irrelevant to the project management realm and pertains to the management of IT at other levels.

One may think that complexity is just another thing that needs to be measured. Shouldn't it simply be better managed, contained and accounted for in project planning?

My experience in corporate IT doesn't support this conclusion. The complexity of the technological environment is frequently underestimated due to a lack of experience, a lack of reliable measures, poor documentation and even a lack of awareness of the mere existence of certain assets. Believe it or not, there are IT assets out there that your own IT employees have limited knowledge about, despite the fact that it's their creation; this is another sign of the magnitude of the complexity issue.

Complexity is not just another reason for project failure to be added to the dozens or hundreds already documented[3][6]. Complexity is a fundamental issue that touches the basic matter of what is created, maintained and managed by your IT team. It's about what has been built: the concrete end result that will be used to support the business. It's about applications, databases or technology devices. It's not about a project.

In project mode, technology assets are created, but as long as what is delivered works, it is assumed correct and goes unchallenged. When the next project comes along, the previously delivered asset is taken as an input to solution design and cost estimation. If the asset is not flexible enough or if it needs to be re-engineered to support the new business requirement, it will simply be factored into the estimates provided to the (potentially unhappy) business sponsor and lost in the obscure enigma of IT costs.

This added complexity is the result of IT decisions and nothing else. It didn't just *happen*. High-impact decisions are made during early project activities as well as very late in project development, sometimes in panic mode. And then there are the smaller decisions that look like they're low-impact but aren't so inconsequential when repeated over and over again.

I myself have been involved in the development and integration of business solutions for three decades now. I've had the chance to witness, sometimes down to the very technical details, the development and implementation of hundreds of business solutions, big and small.

Despite major differences in the nature of the industries, the size of the projects, the constraints, the skills available and the maturity of the organizations, one thing puzzled me and shames me into action: the same architecture and design mistakes that I witnessed in the early years of my career were repeated over the decades and are still being made today.

The errors to which I'm referring are not the small or inconsequential ones, nor are they related to technical style, fashion-of-the-week use of technology or IT-religion warfare. They are significant misconceptions that always lead to the same undesirable outcomes: growth in the complexity of your IT platforms or a solution that lacks agility in the face of future business changes.

The business agility of the IT platforms in which you invest is all about the quality of the output from the IT team that builds them. Lower-quality assets will require more work to change, more time to dismantle and more maintenance staff. In the end, they will become a business-agility boat anchor that pulls you back and away from your objectives.

So why are these decisions made? Why is your IT function now stuck with its own creation: overly complex environments that make it clumsy and impede your agility?

The true root cause is not technical for a second. It has to do with the definition of roles, the measured accountabilities that are given to these roles and their distribution among the personnel.

Digging for Roots

For me, identifying the root causes of the IT dilemma can be likened to the inquisitive nature of a three-year-old. Every answer discovered leads to the question, "Why?" I will not rest until I've gotten to the bottom of it and lucky for you, I have.

To help you understand the fundamental-roles issue, we shall dig into the nature of accountabilities in corporate IT. By the end of Chapter 2, you should get the picture: the same individuals or teams are charged with all aspects of IT, leading to inherent conflicts. These incompatible roles, fuelled by a set of performance measures that favor certain responsibilities to the detriment of others, lead in turn to skewed decision processes. You'll also realize that in the end, the burden is on you, the paying customer.

I will then describe the many ways in which these clashing roles operate to systematically create lower-quality IT assets that result in more complexity. Your corporate IT is stuck in a modus operandi that turns it into a huge machine that constantly creates unwanted convolution. More notably, you will be exposed to the reasons why this occurs:

- IT projects and teams can easily create redundant assets. You'll learn how structure, roles and accountabilities encourage them to do so.

- The speed at which information technologies evolve is by no means an excuse for the creation of unwanted complexity.

- Mergers and acquisitions are falsely cited as causes for unwanted complexity.

- Corporate IT teams create assets that aren't meant to be dismantled in the first place, causing them to be very hard indeed to take apart. You're stuck with what they build for much too long.

- IT budgets are allocated in ways that impede the creation of reusable and flexible components that could better support business agility.

- Budget and urgency are the most frequently cited reasons on the IT floor for cutting corners and delivering inferior-quality assets.

- IT solutions are software-based, virtual in nature and highly malleable, so there's always a way to make things work. But that's a two-edged sword.

- Doing things the right way for maximum business agility takes more time and effort than cutting corners. It benefits external entities, such as the client, but not the project itself.

- Your corporate IT is project-oriented. Therefore, project management logic is applied to all decisions, making them highly skewed toward short-term rewards.

- Your corporate IT is an amalgamation of siloed teams that have all the good or bad reasons to work in a vacuum. They do so because of absent or weak counterbalancing mechanisms.

Don't worry; this isn't happening by design. There's no gigantic conspiracy. Your IT function is doing the best it can within an engagement model that has fundamental flaws in the way that accountabilities are distributed: individuals and teams are charged with incompatible duties.

These conflicting roles have many additional negative impacts on IT's performance, above and beyond the creation of low quality and complexity. We shall go over numerous behavioral pathologies that have lasted for as long as IT has existed and that seem to benefit from no tangible improvement, despite their notoriety. Get ready to learn why:

- Nobody seems to remember anything about past projects, especially when it has to do with questionable design decisions that lead to more complexity and higher project costs.

- The estimation practice in corporate IT shops is outrageously immature, to the point where it should no longer be called a practice.

- Your IT isn't managing business solutions or applications as IT assets. It's geared for managing project budgets as expenses.

- The documentation of million-dollar IT investments is left to the goodwill of individuals whose performance is evaluated in terms of the attainment of short-term objectives. The ability of future generations of IT staff to understand what has been done is considered to be of lesser importance.

- The quality of your assets is scrupulously controlled for all aspects that affect short-term performance, but entire sections of the excellence they deserve are left with little oversight.

- Your corporate IT standards are probably incomplete and surely enforced through anemic processes.

This gloomy portrait of corporate IT is by no means the end of the story. However, "a problem well stated is a problem half solved."[4] The goal of the first volume is to offer a thorough understanding of the issues, their repercussions and most importantly, the reasons behind the unwanted behaviors. Once you've finished Volume 1, I suggest you let it sink in for a few days before you jump into Volume 2. It's my belief that this will help you get the most out of the avenues suggested in the second tome.

With an answer to the "why" question in hand, we'll dive into the "how" in Volume 2. In the second tome as in the first, the solution isn't technical. Basic management and governance strategies for fixing the problems in a permanent and sustainable way will be outlined. The second book is based on the following rationale:

1. You'll never get the business agility and speed you need without corporate IT.

2. Asset inflexibility, unwanted rampant complexity or both will bog down business change.

3. Corporate IT can't speed up without improving the **quality** of its work.

4. Enhancing quality requires managing and evaluating IT **assets** — not just expenses.

5. Revamping asset management and quality control can't happen without a drastic revision of **roles**, decision rights and measured accountabilities.

The distribution of accountabilities is the cornerstone of the problems depicted in this volume as well as the solutions outlined in Volume 2.

---

[4] *This quote, widely attributed to Charles F. Kettering, a renowned engineer and inventor in the first half of the 20th century, is so famous that is has become entrenched in popular parlance. I wasn't able to find a reliable confirmation that he is indeed the author. In any case, the wisdom behind this sentence remains highly relevant to the objective of this first volume.*

The IT staff who support your business have the capacity to improve. After all, it is in their core competencies to analyze complex business problems, dissect them flat on the table and find ways to solve them. It has nothing to do with either skills or effort.

It has to do with what is directly or indirectly expected of them. It has to do with what they're accountable for and evaluated upon. If you change the center of gravity, the whole system will adapt itself, shifting toward new focus points. New behaviors will emerge, while others will subside.

But before we dive into solutions, let's look more closely at what you need to know about corporate IT and were probably never told — although it's likely you had an inkling.

In Chapter 1, we'll make a detour into the construction industry, a required journey in order to fully understand the issues depicted in Chapter 2 and the intimate links they have with the IT-performance measures described in Chapter 3. Chapter 4 will detail how and why your corporate IT basement is caught in a system that makes it a genuine complexity factory. In Chapter 5, you'll come to understand how three types of silos plague corporate IT, fuelling complexity and the production of lower-quality assets. By the time you get through Chapter 6, you'll need no further explanation of the reasons for the poor quality control and quasi-non-existent management of the assets created by your investments in IT. As a bonus, Chapter 7 will explain how the so-called estimation practice is affected by inferior quality, which in turn affects project speed and complexity in an endless loop.

That should give you all the material required, once you let it settle, to be ready for Volume 2.

1. THE TRIANGLE

How a Mature Industry Handles Its Stakeholders' Roles

In 2000, I began major renovations on my house and decided to use the services of an architect — a civil architect of course, not an IT colleague. I became quite attentive to the process the architect went through and the similarities between his approach and my own work experience in the IT world.

One element of affinity was the punctilious rigor the architect applied to determining our needs. He didn't stop at considering the potential solutions we expressed but rather investigated, with more questions, the real requirements. We wanted a solarium, and that desire was the fruit of extensive reflection and discussion on our part. But the architect kept inquiring about how we'd use the space, how we currently went about our days, how we expected to live in 10 years, what the reasons behind the solarium idea were and what our other needs were.

We wanted a better view of the backyard and better access to it. We wanted a bright open space for daytime family living. We wanted a dining room with easy access to the barbecue.

After going through all these true requirements, he came up with a proposal and as you may have guessed, steered us away from the solarium idea. In the end, we built a new wing with floor-to-ceiling windows, but no solarium. It not only suited our needs perfectly, it also added more net square footage, reduced watertightness issues and ultimately brought more value to the property.

Although the nature of the end result in IT is quite different, the requirements-elicitation process takes a similar approach: investigating the processes and expected value while avoiding getting pulled in the wrong direction by preconceived solutions disguised as requirements. As an IT architect, the process I witnessed sounded very familiar.

Another element of affinity was a stepped approach toward the final detailed plans and specifications. After the first requirements-gathering meeting, the architect came back with high-level sketches of our options in order to test our reaction and — I suspect — give us the impression that we had a say in the matter. At each meeting, the drawings focused increasingly on the chosen concept and included more lower-level details. At one point, we had to sign off on the drawings before proceeding into detailed structural, electrical and mechanical blueprints. These precautions, and the method involved, again sounded very familiar to me as an IT architect.

Another similarity was the use of patterns as elements of the design. One example of a pattern is walls meeting at an angle other than 90 degrees. Rooms with windows on two of the four walls is another pattern, as is circular staircases or flooring planks oriented at 45 degrees from the walls. The architect looked at patterns already in place, making sure that an existing pattern's meaning and purpose was respected. He extended or repeated existing patterns while removing useless or conflicting ones. The word "pattern" will ring a bell for IT readers, as it's a commonly used paradigm in IT architectures.[5] I use it daily when acting as an IT architect. There are good patterns, anti-patterns and patterns defined for many types of problems to be solved.

I repeated this experience twice more with different architects, and similar approaches were used both times. This got me thinking about the universal applicability of the solution-design process[6].

Of course, as you delve deeper into the details, the similarities fade. A house is a house and an order capture system is not a house.

IT — with its new and ever-evolving technologies, indisputable youth and very dynamic nature — may yet have more similarities than we think with older and more mature fields. By looking for similarities rather than differences regarding implementation, technology or outcome, we might discover pearls of wisdom applicable to IT. And wisdom I found. Not while I was observing the design process, but later on, when I understood the nature of the roles.

During this renovation experience, the architect was expected to provide, in addition to drawings and specifications, a call for bids package that included all the contractual documents to be signed with the general contractor of our choosing. It is in the latter documents that I found the pearl.

As most legal documents, the contract was filled with precise statements about the responsibilities of the customer, the contractor, subcontractors and their employees, the architecture firm, the engineering firm or any other consulting party. It stipulated who was accountable for following the design documents specifications, conforming to standards, or assessing conformance. It had provisions on how to deal with conformance issues, evaluation of completion, payment schedule and much more.

The spirit of the contractual documents was indisputably to avoid costly misunderstandings about who is responsible and accountable for what. Above all, it had the obvious purpose of protecting the customer.

As a daily witness to several issues that afflict corporate IT performance, specifically when it comes to designing and implementing solutions correctly, I felt compelled to take a closer look at the construction world to better understand how these issues are dealt with.

Here, we'll take a quick detour into the construction industry to show how many of its solutions can be successfully applied to the IT world. Although it would be foolish to think that the construction model could simply be pasted over the IT model thus solving all of our problems[7], I do believe there is much that corporate IT can learn and apply.

To begin with, it is my belief that the construction industry imposes an engagement model that supports clearer communications about issues and a better decision-making process, all leading to higher-quality assets delivered to the customer.
The next pages are by no means intended to be thorough nor authoritative on the construction industry. They are based on my personal observations and research, which began long ago.

---

[5] It is interesting to note that Christopher Alexander, professor of (civil) architecture at Berkeley, wrote books[11][12] about design, city planning, buildings architecture and patterns that have, decades later, almost reached cult status for software-development thought leaders.

[6] Nobel laureate Herbert Simon wrote, "Engineers are not the only professional designers ... Everyone designs who devises courses of action aimed at changing existing situations into preferred ones. Schools of engineering, as well as schools of architecture, business, education, law and medicine, are all centrally concerned with the process of design."[13]

When I was a kid, my father was in charge of public relations for a construction trade newspaper. He spent most of his work weeks meeting with institutional bidders, contractors, associations of all sorts, city inspectors, government agencies and more. In addition to listening to my father's comments about an industry that he knew inside and out, my personal experience and curiosity have led to further research and interviews with civil architects, general contractors and surveyors in order to validate my understanding of their dynamics. My main goal is to unveil an engagement model with patterns of accountability and control that work.

The engagement model is simple: a triangle with three poles of accountability that identify crystal clear roles and several safeguards to ensure that everyone behaves.

The Customer

For the sake of simplicity, we will see the customer as an individual or organization that takes the financial risk of the project and provides the requirements. It could be a future homeowner, a real-estate developer, a private or public organization, a building management corporation that acts as a delegate for an investor, etc.

The role of the customer is to provide the investment money and the requirements.

Requirements can be living or usage requirements, but also financial prescriptions, such as the expected return on investment (ROI) once the units are sold, or the expected rental revenue model. There can also be timing requirements due

---

[7] Because of the fundamental nature of what is built, and also because of the major differences that exist in the design process, especially the delineation between when design ends and construction starts[37].

to dependencies with other projects or events, such as the planned demolition of an old warehouse or the home purchasing peak season.

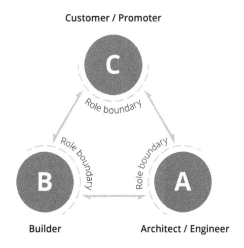

Figure 1 - Role Delineation in the Construction Industry

The customer can be a seasoned developer or an international investment corporation with vertical integration, but most of the time — and for the sake of the parallel we're drawing with the IT industry — assume that the customer has very little knowledge of construction techniques, projects, laws or the dynamics of the industry.

The customer's objective is to maximize the ROI, whether this return is sales, rent, property value, family happiness, or social pride.

The Architect

The architect is an individual or a team that has all the educational and legal credentials required by law to practice the profession and has been hired by the customer. There are several contractual options for compensation, but the most important point for our analysis is that the customer pays the architect.

The main role of the architect is to gather the customer's requirements, translate them into construction requirements and express them in a form that efficiently supports validating, estimating, calling for bids and signing construction contracts.

In short, the architect defines what has to be built. Through their education and experience, architects also act as consultants to the customer on layouts, materials, construction techniques, visual effects, aging effects, future maintenance, applicable rules and regulations, and estimating the relative costs of various options.

In some cases, the architect can be hired by the customer as an intermediary to the construction firms for the tasks of calling for bids, analyzing responses and providing recommendations. Additionally, the architect — the same or a different one — can be hired for worksite inspection in order to validate that what is effectively built respects drawings and specifications, codes and standards. The architect can also be hired to present, defend and obtain city or other governmental permits required for construction.

The architect is not an engineer and therefore has the responsibility to advise the customer if one is needed to perform a more detailed analysis and design for areas that fall outside the scope of architecture work. However, for our purposes, let's assume the role "architect" includes all design professions required to prepare the drawings and specifications, including engineers, interior designers, landscape designers, etc.

The architect's objectives are to secure the contract and maximize customer satisfaction, while limiting the time spent on the project in order to remain profitable. The architect works in a competitive environment where reputation is a differentiating factor.

The Builder

The builder is a generic term for the person who represents all the parties involved in the actual physical construction of the project. The builder is epitomized by the general contractor, his employees and all the specialty subcontractors required to perform the work.

The builder takes the drawings and specifications as input and provides estimated (or fixed) costs to be used as a contractual basis. When the project starts, he manages the execution and logical sequence of activities, the involvement of staff and subcontractors, the procurement of materials and supplies, the smooth running of the worksite, and compliance to the specified or applicable codes and laws, such as worksite safety or environmental regulations. It goes without saying that most of the investment money goes to the builder and most risks will materialize during or after the builder's involvement.

The builder's main objectives are to secure the contract with an attractive price during the bidding process and maximize profit during execution. The builder works in a highly competitive industry where all costs are fairly well known in advance and where the differentiating factor is price.

To achieve profitability, the builder must have a relentless focus on materials cost, manpower and operating efficiency, as well as skills, techniques or tools that maximize productivity. Quality must be just enough to comply to specifications and standards in order to avoid costly rework.

Functions and Frictions

Antagonisms Between Stakeholders
in the Construction Industry Do Exist.

These three stakeholders, although quite different in their roles, backgrounds and objectives, must work together in the most harmonious way possible in order for the endeavour to be a success for everyone.

This triangle is filled with colliding intentions or perceptions that can make this fruitful collaboration less than ideal. These frictions are depicted here for a very good reason: they bare a disturbing similarity with analogous tensions observed in the corporate IT world.

The customer may be reluctant to use the services of an architect. After all, architects have the highest hourly wages of all building trades. If he knows exactly what he wants, the customer could hire a talented technician, tell him what is needed, and save some good money. If that is not an option, some contractors may say they have their own architects and can do the same work at a lower price, or better, have it included in the price!

The customer, especially if not well-versed in construction theory or practice, may have a paranoid feeling that the builder will do everything to cut corners or try to turn any legitimate request into a contract amendment. This feeling might be exacerbated if the chosen contractor had a lower price tag than the others, leading the customer to fear the builder voluntarily low-balled his price to get the contract and will do everything to get his profit back.

The builder may view the customer as being fussy about irrelevant details that do not change the quality of the work being done. He may also view customers as unremittingly asking for "little things" that become free extras for which they are never paid.

The builder can also have mixed feelings about the architecture profession, which he may see as filled with arugula-fed intellectuals who can't even drive a nail into a two-by-four. They often feel that architects come up with blueprints that are full of holes in need of correction or designs that just don't make sense. To top it off, they come back as worksite inspectors and count the screws on wall boards!

Architects have their own tensions with customers who never have the money to fulfill their ambitions, always change their minds and are very hard to find when the time comes to sign-off on final documents.

The architect is often in conflict with the builder, not only when defects are uncovered, but also because the builder sometimes changes the design or specifications without the architect's approval, with or without direct dealings with the customer. The architect knows the builder's tricks to save time, effort and money at the expense of quality, and his experience has shown him that some builders are likely to resort to this.

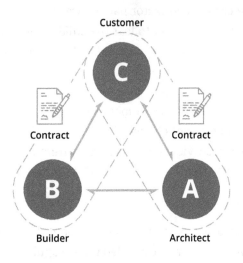

Figure 2 - Contractually Bound Roles

In addition, many architects see themselves as the only stakeholder who understands the artistic dimension of buildings or what it takes to create a living space that will bring about admiration and recognition.

There is one crucial point that I must repeat about roles in the construction industry: however antagonistic these roles may be, and regardless of each individial's skills and aspirations, the responsibilities of each party are clear and understood by all.

Errors Happen in Construction, Too

When Things Go Awry in the Construction Industry, Roles Are Rarely an Issue.

My recent interest in the world of construction has triggered interesting discussions with professionals from the industry, and as in any other field, it's clear that unwanted things happen.

Of course, human nature being what it is, the first reflex is often to blame others. However, in the construction industry there is a fundamental difference in identifying where the problem is and who is responsible and should pay for it; the basic roles and responsibilities depicted in the sections above are never questioned.

Let's take a scenario where the customer makes a mid-project worksite visit and is furious to see that the fireplace is in the master bedroom instead of the living room. Investigations begin to find out more. The livid customer points his finger either at the architect who did not listen to his instructions or at the contractor who he believes can't read blueprints.

The drawings are put on the table to see that indeed, the fireplace is drawn in the bedroom. The contractor breathes more freely, but beads of sweat can now be seen on the architect's forehead. The problem now lies between the customer and the architect.

The customer pulls from his briefcase early drawings that clearly show the fireplace in the living room, as he ordered. But the final blueprints, the ones reviewed and signed by the customer, have the fireplace at the other end of the condo. So whose fault is it?

The customer could argue that a fireplace does not change places like that and that he was not looking for such a defect when signing the final blueprints, but rather making sure that the latest changes were included.

The architect could argue that the reason she asks for signatures is to avoid this type of unfortunate error or she may argue that the early drawings do not carry her seal or signature.

Fortunately, before the situation degenerates into a legal battle, the contractor comes back and proposes that, since the living room is far from finished, he could build an angle wall and put in a second fireplace, for an unbeatable price. The customer concedes, as it adds some value to the condo, the contractor gets more business, and the architect promises to give the customer free design hours on the next construction project that she hopes to sign with him.

This scenario has a nice ending. It could have been worse. But one very important observation comes into play: the respective responsibilities of each party are never questioned.

If the design documents are wrong, the architect is at fault. If the customer signs off on something without looking or asks for something that he later regrets, he's at fault. If the contractor puts the blueprints upside down on the wall or does not do the proper quality checks on his crew's work, he's at fault.

When errors happen in the construction industry, while there is some room for interpretation, roles and responsibilities are never in question.

The Wisdom of Safeguards

How Good Behavior Is Framed and Fenced by Institutionalized Reminders.

The above-mentioned tensions among the main stakeholders will certainly create a *déjà vu* feeling for the readers involved in IT projects.

What inspires me is how the construction industry deals with this: by openly recognizing the differences in roles and putting in place a structure that keeps these roles delineated, framed and safeguarded from natural or malicious deviations.

Let's look at some of these mechanisms.

Firstly, there are clear boundaries between the three main roles that are not just a gentlemen's agreement or some natural polarization of activities after thousands of years of trial and error: they are contractually and legally defined.

Looking at standard construction document templates[14], the roles are laser cut, with clear definitions including descriptions of the authority and accountability of each role. And to ensure there are no ambiguities, certain templates specify what certain roles are not accountable for.

Even customers know exactly what is expected of them, such as the approval of documents and change orders, access to the site, performing of surveys, getting city permits, etc., as well as what the consequences are for unreasonable delays.

But in the end and above all the subtleties, the roles are clear and indisputable: the customer pays, decides and owns, the architect defines and checks, and the contractor builds.

Secondly, there are extensive industry-wide competency management mechanisms. Architects must have a stamp and blueprints must be stamped. It is illegal under certain conditions to use unstamped documents. In order to have the right to stamp blueprints and specifications, an architect must be a member in good standing of the professional order that has authority over the territory where the project is performed (Figure 3).

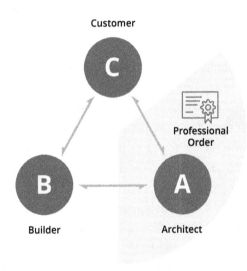

Figure 3 - Lawful Orders for Professional Conduct

For public projects, the government agencies that sign construction contracts are lawfully obligated to use the services of architects. For all customers, the local agencies that issue construction permits require architect involvement for projects of a certain size or complexity.

The legislator of the applicable constituency imbeds in duly voted laws the authority of the professional order (architects or engineers) to define applicable diplomas, identify schools that can issue degrees, define internship requirements, conduct skills exams, define and impose to its members a professional code of ethics, conduct practice investigations, manage complaints, impose fines or even revoke the right to practice (Figure 3).

These codes of conduct[15] are written with an obvious inclination toward protecting the customer. One interesting point is the importance given to the management of conflicts of interest: professionals must declare any related participation, including employment or other involvement, with builders. Obedience to the code of professional ethics and conduct transcends employment or contract waivers.

Builders must also show proof of competence (Figure 5). Contractor licences are required in order to receive construction permits and licensing requires passing exams to test adequate knowledge of safety, environmental, legal or business practices. Specialized construction trades, such as electricians or plumbers, must have their specific licenses to practice. Practicing without a permit or a license means legal trouble.

Thirdly, the construction industry has an extensive set of documented and enforced standards (Figure 4). The codes cover farms, buildings, residential houses, framework, plumbing, electricity and insulation, to name a few.

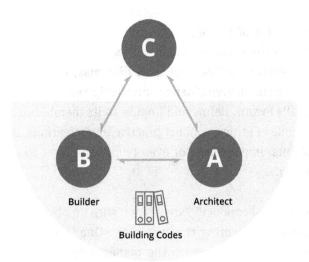

Figure 4 - Standardization Through Building

A builder or an architect can rarely "invent" a new way to do something, unless it is analyzed, tested, approved and eventually included in the code. Compliance to standards is contractually and legally enforced.

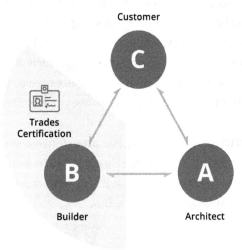

Figure 5 - Management of Skills for Construction Trades

Architecture specifications simply refer to the applicable standards, assuming that the builder is cognizant and up-to-date.

Finally, projects must be submitted to governance bodies that have the right to deny permission and usually hire inspectors that have legal authority to inspect and demand corrective action in case of noncompliance (Figure 7). In addition, the customer can also hire third-party inspectors or reuse the architect (Figure 6) to ensure conformance to plans, codes and regulations.

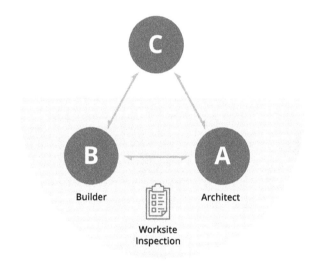

Figure 6 - Architect Used as Worksite Inspector

All these safeguards have been put in place over time to control deviant behaviors and promote higher levels of quality, all to the benefit of the customer or the public in general.

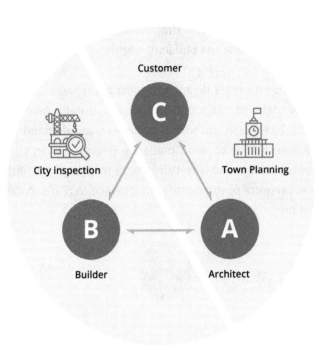

Figure 7 - Standards Compliance for Plans and Execution

Although the severity of consequences for poor quality in the construction industry are greater than those found in corporate IT, the structure, roles and accountabilities should at least be inspirational[16].

In corporate IT, while we may not build tunnels or skyscrapers, we are spending millions of dollars on projects year after year. Drawing a parallel between roles and accountabilities should enlighten your understanding of some foundational issues within your IT team, as we shall see in the next chapter.

CHAPTER ONE TAKEAWAYS

- *The centuries-old construction industry has grown into a 3-poled roles structure: the Customer, the Architect and the Builder.*

- *These roles are well-delineated and never challenged, even when things go awry.*

- *Interplay between the major stakeholders is framed by independent bodies to ensure that boundaries are not crossed and that regulations — including quality standards — are followed.*

- *The whole structure is ostensibly aimed at protecting the Customer and the public in general.*

2. THE GEOMETRY OF IT

How the Corporate IT Engagement Model Creates Conflicts of Roles

Mapping IT roles to the three poles found in the construction industry's engagement model made perfect sense to me due to their obvious similarities. The IT roles that I had either held myself or worked with over the last few decades smoothly fall into one of the same three broad categories described in the last chapter: customer, builder and architect. Names may differ a bit, but they share the same common objectives and the same antagonistic positions.

However, as you will see in the next few pages, there are structural differences in IT's assigned roles and accountabilities that are not always for the benefit of the paying customer. Let's begin with a review of the major roles and then we'll dive into how they engage in delivering your IT business solutions.

The IT Customer

In IT, as in the construction world, there is a customer. If we retain the same definition — the individual who defines the requirements, pays for the endeavour and owns the final product — the customer will usually be a senior manager or executive from a non-IT line of business. There are cases when a given project is sponsored and paid for by the IT function, for example when integrating a new IT help desk application, but let's keep it simple and coherent with the vast majority of business solution developments.

The customer, then, is typically a vice president or equivalent for a given sector of the organization. This customer has funds available to perform some changes in the organization that involve information technology support. The funding was most probably granted by an investment committee, based on a business case that showed tangible returns for such a change or major risks for not doing it.

The customer often delegates responsibilities, especially for the requirements definition, to one or more lieutenants and provides higher-level oversight on schedule and budget, as well as support for strategic-level issues resolution.

The IT Architect

Unless the project is very small, the architect is in fact a set of designers who can be part of the same team or split into different IT organizational units.

Architects rarely cover all aspects of the design process, and as such, are specialized vertically (from high level to very detailed designs), horizontally (taking care of specific applications or business functions) or by some other technical strata (infrastructure, data, application, etc.).

Because there is not yet a professional order in IT that defines a cross-industry education curriculum or the exact scope of responsibilities, there may be significant differences between what an architect does in your IT organization versus the one across the street.

Like many other things in IT, we are still awaiting true professional standards[8]. In the meantime, the definition of the work and responsibilities of an architect is somewhat elastic and the labels vary from one place to another, often leaving other stakeholders, including you, the customer, dubious about the exact role of the architect.

Three important observations need to be made about architecture roles: (1) all of these roles are focused on *defining* the solution, not building it. In other words, the work they perform is design work only; (2) the individuals performing these roles are usually spread across the IT organization; and (3) a very important last observation: many of these design roles work in the same teams that build, deliver and maintain the solution.

The IT Builder

Just as in the construction world, IT builders are teams of people who effectively forge the solution. This includes programmers (nowadays called web developers, app developers, etc.), as well as testers, help editors, analysts, development tools specialists, code librarians, user experience specialists and many others. The IT builder manages a variety of skills that resemble to the construction trades.

---

[8] *There are nevertheless efforts to get there, and the IT industry is not staying still on the subject. The Open Group for example, is defining architecture standards and providing professional certifications for IT architects[40].*

The builders take their fair share of the total cost of a business solution. One important point is that, contrary to the construction world, it is sometimes difficult to distinguish between designers and builders, and in many areas of IT construction, the person responsible for creating something is also responsible for performing some sort of design.

Functions and Frictions 2.0
Antagonisms Between Stakeholders in Corporate IT Also Exist.

In the previous chapter I took some time to explain points of view, antagonisms and colliding interests between the three poles of the construction industry engagement model.

Here, too, the customer, who is not IT-fluent, may feel that he is being hoaxed by the builder who turns every issue into a change order, sucking more money out of his pocket.

Much like in construction, the IT architect and builder may become irritated by customers who don't know what they want or simply don't understand the problem that needs to be solved.

The customer, who may not always understand the technically-obscure dispatching of IT roles, can be left wondering what an architect is doing and why he's paying for work that does not seem to yield tangible outputs.

The IT builder, who has been building for years, is convinced that she knows what and how to deliver, and doesn't need an architect to tell her what to do. If she believes that architecture is in fact required, she is convinced that she can do it herself. Antagonistic positions are not an issue *per se*. I see them as normal and even healthy when framed properly. What is an issue, and a major one, however, is that in IT, contrary to the construction industry, almost all the safeguards are missing. There are no signed contracts that clearly define the roles. There are no building codes and very little cross-industry standards. There are no professional codes of conduct ratified by government agencies. There are no trade certification cards to be shown on a worksite and there are no penalties in case of noncompliance.

In IT, more than any other engineering field, anyone can play any role with little immediate effect. The organizational impact of all this leeway is that major roles are rarely clear. The corporate IT engagement model has a propensity for conflicts of roles and a very shaky conception of segregation of duties. And that leads us to the next section.

Where Is my Triangle?
How the Corporate IT Engagement Model Puts Too Many Conflicting Accountabilities on the Same Teams and Individuals.

Let's first compare the typical engagement model of the construction industry with that of IT. This exercise will help us better understand where the triangle has gone.

Figure 8 depicts a typical engagement situation in the construction industry. The customer hires an architect and later selects a builder.

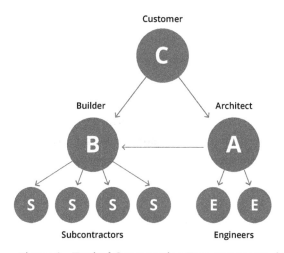

Figure 8 - Typical Construction Engagement Model

This usually happens in a sequence, hiring the architect first and then, with the help of the architect's specification documents and drawings, selecting the builder. The architect then interacts with the builder to provide guidance or additional information on the specifications, or if the customer wishes, acts as a worksite inspector.

There is also another engagement situation — the "turnkey" option — where the selected general contractor offers all the services including architecture (see Figure 9). This model is quite important to mention because it resembles, in a way, the IT situation in most large organizations, but at first sight only. The main difference is that the *safeguards* I briefly described in Chapter 1 still apply in the construction industry, even in a turnkey situation. Over and above the main stakeholders, there are still independent and impartial authorities that take care of skills, professional conduct, conflicts of interest and compliance to standards and regulations. None of the construction roles can bypass laws and regulations, and they are all subject to inspection by several external bodies that have no vested interest in the project.

If we now take a closer look at the typical engagement model for the implementation of an IT business solution in a large organization, there are several important differences to note.

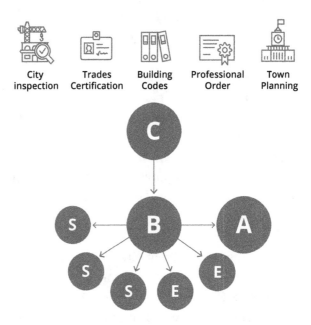

City inspection   Trades Certification   Building Codes   Professional Order   Town Planning

Figure 9 - Turnkey Engagement Model for Construction

First, the IT customer does not engage with the architect. For a business decision-maker with his own business to run, understanding the internal workings of the IT function is not a priority, and as such IT is usually viewed as a whole. The customer engages with "IT," period.

The main point of contact, once the project start date arrives, will be an IT manager, a project manager or a program manager. Whatever the name, the main role of that person is to get to the finish line: a working solution. In other words, the IT customer deals directly and exclusively with the IT builder.

The second obvious difference is the relative confinement of the customer with respect to IT. In the construction industry, customers can deal with whichever architect they wish, based on references or on satisfactory past experiences with that same architect.

For customers who are regulated, such as government agencies, an architecture contest or a call for bids may be mandatory. The same applies for choosing the builder. With the construction industry being much more standardized, architects and builders are more interchangeable than those in the IT business. The complexity of IT systems portfolios in large organizations is such that knowing and understanding it is in itself quite a challenge, even for internal experts.

Although there are frequent cases where external vendors are contracted for business solutions, when it comes to providing core applications and/or integrating the solution into the customer's environment, the vast majority of IT solution projects are handed over to the internal IT function.

The third difference is this: the external regulating mechanisms found in the construction industry are internal to IT, not external. This disparity has major impacts on quality.

For IT, the equivalent of construction codes and standards are either developed in-house or adopted from external bodies, but nevertheless are assessed for compliance internally.

The required skills for IT builders or IT architects are not regulated by an external body that grants — or denies — the ability of the IT resource to work. Each IT organization defines its own set of academic education standards or required professional certifications, when defined at all. A professional order or code of conduct for IT architects backed-up by civil laws simply does not exist.

A picture being worth a thousand words, take a look at Figure 10 that shows the resulting engagement model for most business solutions development projects.

If this typical IT engagement model were implemented in the construction industry, the builders would not only build the solution, but would also provide architecture services, define the industry standards, do city planning, define and manage trade orders, and play the inspector role. But it wouldn't stop there: the builder would become ruler over a mighty monopoly, providing everything, including water, power and public road maintenance!

This is the reality of corporate IT engagement in most organizations today.

The corporate customer relies on IT not only to build the solution, but also to design it, define the corporate standards and ensure compliance to design and quality criteria.

As if this isn't enough, the builder is also responsible for running all the applications smoothly, for protecting networks and data from malicious attacks, for guaranteeing service levels of availability and response time, and for all other operational duties related to information technologies.

We are finally getting to the gist of it: your organization is giving several incompatible duties to its internal IT function and putting it in a difficult position of carrying out these conflicting roles.

Many of these roles are mutually exclusive by their very nature. They cannot all be under the same hat, worn by a single individual or single team. It just cannot work, at least not to the best interest of the paying customer. The concept of segregation of duties exists in many other fields, but for some reasons, it hasn't hit some key areas of corporate IT yet.

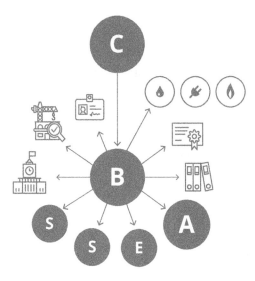

**Figure 10 - The Typical IT Engagement Model
Applied to Construction**

This clashing of roles has a direct impact on the systematic creation of ever bigger, convoluted, more complex IT systems. This is not caused by an eternal state of immaturity in the IT industry, nor by external factors to your own IT function. As we shall see in the coming chapters, there are many questionable behaviors in corporate IT that are rooted in these conflicting roles.

The Hijacked Architecture

How the Architect Role is Usurped by the Builder, leaving No One Accountable.

In the IT geometry, there is no such thing as a triangle. The customer deals with the builder, who takes care of everything. There is still a need to understand the requirements, and design that has to be delivered to the customer. But the clear delineation between the architect and the builder is absent. Equally absent is the direct link between the paying customer and the architect. Since the main responsibility of the Builder is to deliver the solution, the identity of who is responsible for designing is hidden behind the builder and the accountability becomes ambiguous or absent.

In my career, I hope that I have seen it all: projects without architects, improvised architects with skills issues, true architects without any architecting accountability, architects left to themselves with no organizational support, IT managers architecting, project managers architecting, customers architecting, programmers architecting. And these are not point-in-time cases that once happened: they are the norm rather than the exception and I have seen this happening on an almost regular basis. Whatever the scenario, one thing stood out: no one is ever really liable for the quality of the architecture in front of a paying customer.

The Geometry Exam Results

In the End, the Customer Pays For Everything, Including the Perverse Effects of a Skewed Engagement Model.

You now have a sense of the profound structural issues in the corporate IT engagement model. There are too many clashing responsibilities within the same team. There is little effective segregation of duties between those who define what to do, those who do it and those that check what has been done.

You, the customer, you are left with a single desk to go to, with no healthy counterweight mechanisms. That leads to areas of IT being neglected. Not because your IT teams don't care, but because they are caught in an engagement model where they have no other choice but to work on what seems the most important.

The good news is that it can be changed. In the next chapter we will first get an understanding of what is vital to IT staff by looking at what is measured.

CHAPTER TWO TAKEAWAYS

- *There are equivalent client, architect and builder duties in corporate IT that share the same objectives as the construction industry.*

- *In corporate IT we can put in place the missing safeguards to frame role boundaries and compliance to quality standards of any sort.*

- *There are several areas of opportunity for improving the segregation of duties in corporate IT and substantially reducing conflicting roles.*

3. ACCOUNTABILITY THROUGH MEASURES

How IT Quantitative Performance Measures Reinforce Certain Accountabilities and Weaken Others

For the first half of my career I was always uncomfortable with yearly performance evaluations. There were several reasons for this, apart from the fact that these evaluations had a direct impact on my career and the hard cash bonus attached. First, I had this uneasy feeling about being judged. I simply couldn't swallow the patriarchal work relationship between an employee and a boss. Second, I was unnerved by personal interpretations of my performance based on anecdotes and qualitative evaluation of months of labor, or worse, quantitatively reported performance based on mere impressions instead of quantitative data.

At some point, I discovered that when performance was based on real numbers, things went smoother. Everything was clearer, both from an expectations point of view, as well as interpretation of my results. There was simply less to interpret, which in turn lessened the uneasy feeling about being judged. As a manager, I came to realize that when expectations were based on quantitative metrics, things went smoother, too.

The downside is that measuring takes time and effort; you need to collect data, store it, track it and report on it. My bosses, my employees and I were therefore never keen on collecting performance data for things that weren't that important.

What Really Counts

In Corporate IT, What Is Measured Quantitatively Becomes What Matters: Systems Stability and Performance, and On-Time, On-Budget Delivery of Changes.

If you want to know what's really important for any corporate function, just look at the hard-numbered performance measures in place.

What makes your senior IT staff shine? To which IT-specific performance metrics are their yearly bonuses linked? What will make your CIO stay for longer than the average four years in service?[22] What type of counter performance from IT senior management would be a valid trigger for dismissal?

IT performance indicators have a major impact on how the IT function organizes itself. These indicators determine what will be the main areas of focus for people and processes.

Non-measured or non-quantitatively measured performance indicators are a sign of neglected areas of IT, while systematically and quantitatively measured indicators are signs of areas that are top priority.

My experience in the trenches clearly confirms this. Any aspect of the job that directly touches a personal, quantitatively measured performance indicator will get done. Not only will it get done, but IT personnel will put processes and tools in place to support improved effectiveness.

Now, having work priorities is not an issue in and of itself. The problem lies in the cases where the same person or team has responsibility for incompatible areas. The quantitatively measured objectives will always be favored at the expense of the rest and that's when unwanted behaviors emerge.

Without any knowledge of your IT organization, I can guess which two categories of key performance indicators (KPIs) are at the top of the list for your IT function.

In all IT organizations, the number one area of responsibility, with clear and direct accountabilities, is operational stability and performance.

This first category is usually called the "Keep the lights on" (KTLO) or "Run the engine" indicators that aim at measuring IT operational performance on the existing systems or services.

This will include measures of the availability of major systems, the number and duration of the outages (when the IT systems were not available), the average response time on important applications, measures of average network throughput, and many other highly technical and quantitative gauges.

These are the fundamentals of any IT department, and as such, the expected performance is quite precise, leaving very little room for interpretation. If the IT organization fails in these aspects, things will either have to change very rapidly or people will face repercussions.

Consequently, the metrics are strictly quantitative and reported on a regular basis: minutes of downtime per month, number of outages, number of seconds for processing a given transaction and the like.

If IT fails in this area, heads will roll. If critical systems are down for half a day, it better be a case of force majeure or else some IT team members should get very nervous about their jobs. This clearly reveals the significance of this responsibility.

The second most important category of performance indicators is related to "project delivery." As explained in Chapter 2, projects are the main conduits for implementing new IT strategies or supporting business change.

There are many ways to measure a project's success. The more you dive into project management science and hands-on knowledge, the more you realize that although there are different perceptions of project success, there are only three basic measures of performance for project delivery.

This trio of performance measures is universally recognized, taught and documented, and almost systematically measured and reported in IT organizations: time, cost and scope[9].

---

[9] *Project performance is more than time, scope and budget, but these are the fundamental ones. They are clearly defined in the PMBoK[42], and although complete books are dedicated to the measurement of projects[41], they remain the crucial ones.*

Table 1
Quantitative Measures of the Top Performance Expectations

IT Performance Area	Typical Indicators	Measures	Units	Precision
Operational stability and efficiency (KTLO)	System stability	Percentage of operational time window when systems are available for use	%	Hundredths or thousandths of a percentage point
		Number of critical system outages	Count	Count per month
	System response time	Time required for system response on critical functions	Seconds	Tenths of a second
	System stability	Number of critical system errors and crashes	Count	Count per month/day
	Time required to perform critical IT processes	Time for replacement employee laptop	Hours	Hours & minutes
		Average wait time for the IT help desk	Seconds	Average count
Efficiency in managing major changes (OTOB)	Project on-time	Amount of time before/after planned completion date	Calendar days	Count of days
	Project on-budget	Percentage over or under planned budget	%	Units of percentage points

The time measure translates into the attainment of the scheduled milestones or important dates of delivery. The cost measure transposes into how much funds were effectively needed compared to the planned budget. The scope, which is sometimes mingled with the concept of quality, is a measure of what was effectively delivered compared to what was planned or defined. But in the case of IT business solutions, measuring scope or quality is a challenge, and it is an even greater challenge to compare it to what was planned.

Early budgets and schedules are usually determined with very little knowledge of the requirements or the architecture of the end solution. Whether or not a given IT solution provides a given function or business performance is subject to debate and interpretation. Compared to other industries where scope is measured in square footage or compliance to detailed specifications, an IT business solution's scope attainment is hard to grasp.

In the end, what remain are the hard, measurable numbers that make a clear statement about performance and leave little space for controversy: on-time and on-budget (OTOB).

Depending on your organization, schedule may be viewed as more important than cost, or the other way around, but in all cases they come at the top.

Take a look at Table 1 where I have put typical performance measures. You recognize that the criteria are grouped in the two main objectives: KTLO and OTOB. One striking point about the table is that the accountabilities are quantitatively measured; not by approximate measures, but rather by highly precise gauges, which in some cases are down to decimal fractions! Also remarkable, all of these metrics use standardized units of measure applicable to all possible cases. They are easy to understand, both from the side that delivers (IT) and the side that pays (you). Universality and the quantification of the measures of performance both indicate the importance of any given accountability. One last important observation, albeit less obvious, is that these measures are easily auditable. You could decide to have these metered by independent parties to avoid that the counting party isn't also the one that is being evaluated.

In your organization, there are certainly other gauges in place, but how do they measure against the ones above in terms of business criticality? Are they qualitatively evaluated or hard-numbered? Are they related to IT accountabilities or general measures applied to all functions? My guess is that the really important stuff is what is closely related to the table above: flawless execution in support of the operations, and managing change within planned budgets and time frames.

There are of course other counter-performance issues that could lead to dismissal, such as skill retention issues or leadership problems, but the table above deals only with the core accountabilities that apply exclusively to the IT function.

Figure 11 eloquently shows the importance of what is expected of corporate IT. On one side, the most important responsibilities, KTLO and OTOB, are quantitatively measured and career impact of failure is high. All other expectations, "The Rest", are left to qualitative measures — when measured — and have a job-keeping impact on IT staff of a lesser magnitude.

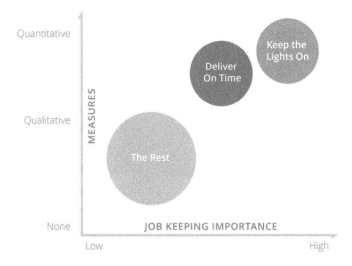

Figure 11 - Classifying Performance Measures for IT

One last important detail to remember is that project performance is evaluated for a given fiscal year only. What happened last year is promptly forgotten and next year's projects are not yet on the radar. Hence any project-related aspect that has an impact on future projects is rarely measured.

This is no small detail, for the majority of IT's most important performance measures are either immediate (operational measures) or for the current year (project delivery measures) and this has a very palatable impact on some behaviors within IT teams.

The lack of hard-numbered performance gauges in many areas[40] has nothing to do with the difficulty of measuring long-term impact or more elusive quality criteria. Remember that your IT team provides your business with whatever performance measures you need in order to thrive and beat the competition. If you ask them to measure something, anything you can imagine, they will salute, say, "Yes ma'am," and will find a way to give you monthly, weekly and daily reports showing whatever numbers you require. That's an IT core competency. Collecting, storing, processing and presenting data is what IT folks have worked on their entire careers.

If you think that the set of quantitative measures collected and presented by your IT team looks a bit emaciated, it is not due to a lack of know-how.

Because the IT engagement model places all responsibilities on a single function, priorities must be set. Hence, a focus is placed on measured areas where positive or negative repercussions are high. And then there's The Rest.

Third and Close to Nothingness
Many Other Virtues of IT Work Are Left Unmeasured, and at the Mercy of Good Intentions.

Much as clear and quantified performance metrics for IT operations and projects signify their importance, the absence of quantified measures for other areas of IT signify of their inconsequence.

So how do the intrinsic qualities of the tangible work outputs of corporate IT get measured? For example, what about adaptability to change, compliance to standards, or maintainability of delivered assets? How about speed? What about quality? Isn't IT delivering tangible "stuff" that should be counted, trended and compared, like any other corporate function?

Even speed itself, the ultimate performance criterion that you should expect from your IT function in these times of rapid market disruptions, is not present in that table[23].

Why aren't these other elements represented in the table above?

They are absent, along with the many other expectations that you may have in mind, because the conflicting accountabilities of the usual corporate IT engagement model push them to third — and far behind these two categories — regardless of their innate virtues. In 25 years, I have never seen such metrics. Any attempts that I have witnessed were promptly nipped in the bud due to lack of motivated IT sponsors. Response to business change translates to projects delivered. Quality transposes to existing assets running smoothly.

In other words, the agility of your investments is left to good intentions. It falls into The Rest, close to irrelevant, down in the lower left quadrant in Figure 11.

Attainment of agility and speed is impeded by two interrelated roadblocks. As we just learned, there is a lack of quantitative measures to help steer IT behaviors. But conflicting roles make it harder for IT to succeed in this area. These blockers work together: colliding roles impede measuring IT's performance with respect to quality or business agility and conversely, the absence of quantitative measures reduces the tool set available to those in charge of attaining such objectives.

By no means am I suggesting that such flexibility in IT assets does not exist because it is systematically and voluntarily blocked. Resilient, reusable and flexible solutions can be built, but IT teams — and especially the architects and designers — are structurally challenged in their quest for imbedding in the solutions the qualities that will make this happen.

Architects responsible for defining what needs to be done are working, either directly or indirectly, for the same team that delivers projects. They work for the Builder, who is quantitatively measured for being OTOB. As we will see in Chapter 5, any quality criterion that does not help attaining OTOB objectives becomes an impediment to attain them — a cruel dichotomy. There are obvious limits in the architect's capacity to demand that the right designs be used. Even with clear responsibilities, there remains an obvious subordination link, either within the project or in the overall IT organizational structure.

In my experience, when true high-quality assets are created, it is a result of exceptional conditions, including chance, hidden agendas, superhuman efforts or the presence of remarkably skilled people.

If your organization is spending tens or hundreds of millions of dollars in new IT business solutions year after year, would you rely on chance and superheroes, or rather on clear accountabilities and repeatable processes that foster, in a sustainable way, the attainment of the objective?

After next chapter, you will fathom the extent to which clashing accountabilities kill business agility by systematically creating an evermore complex web of lower quality IT assets.

CHAPTER THREE TAKEAWAYS

- *In corporate IT, as in any other field, true priorities can be distinguished by the nature of the personal and team performance measures.*

- *The most important, controlled and monitored IT capacities are those that are quantitatively measured.*

- *The IT function is notably and quantitatively measured in two broad areas: (1) operations stability and performance; and (2) efficiency in managing change.*

- *You can significantly boost agility and speed of IT by quantitatively measuring the key innate virtues of the delivered solutions.*

4. THE COMPLEXITY FACTORY

How Accountabilities Make Corporate IT a Giant Complexity Generating Machine

How many cars do you own? One, two, three? Unless you're a fan or a collector, you probably think like me: one automobile is very practical, but trouble increases for every additional car. If you own five cars, it's five times the maintenance, the insurance, the repairs, the licensing, the parking spaces, etc.

Now suppose — just for fun — that each of your cars needed a different mechanic and there was no way that one of the mechanics could work on more than one car. Also suppose that the mechanics need to work on a full-time basis, directly for you and no one else. In addition, pretend (just for fun, although this is getting less and less amusing) that there are no auto parts available, and that each mechanic needs to have access to a manned machine shop to manufacture the parts required for repairs or maintenance. You would be the proud owner of five cars, five machine shops and managing lots of employees. In other words, you'd be really motivated to own only one car.

In the virtual world of IT, this is the way things operate. And to make it worse, it is very hard getting rid of what you own and I grossly oversimplified things with this car analogy.

The more an IT platform is left to grow organically and ungoverned, the faster entropy starts prying into it. That's when integration challenges arise and become a burden to business agility. In our evermore digitalized world, new business integrations are key elements of success[10]. They are however based on IT and anything that impairs making new things work with the existing ones slows down change endeavors. Complexity or inflexibility of the technology environments already in place is a critical one.

If you know or feel that your organization is being weighed down by far too many assets or inflexible platforms, know that you are not alone. But this is not due to some unavoidable degradation or an eternal state of immaturity. This situation is rooted in IT architecture and design decisions, the small ones and the strategic ones, all leading to the current state of your IT portfolio.

In the next pages, we will go over the mechanisms that create unwanted complexity: unnecessary replication of components, nonstandard work, and hard to change or to remove designs.

To ensure you do not get fooled by some long-standing excuses from corporate IT, we'll also cover usual suspects that are, in my view, terrible justifications: mergers and acquisitions, the speed of changes in technology, and urgency.

But before we start, you need to grasp something of the utmost importance that has a huge impact on time, costs and the issues depicted in this book. It has to do with the true qualities of a working IT solution. So let's begin there...

---

[10] *According to leading edge field research results, integration is no less than "[...] the basis for competition in the digital economy."[20]*

In the End It Always Works

Why a Working IT Solution Should Not Be Taken For More Than What It Is.

Business IT solutions are mainly made of software and software has characteristics that are hard to find anywhere else: it is highly flexible and malleable, to a point where you can do almost anything. It is, in its most basic substance, a series of electrical impulses representing numbers. All a computer does is compute numbers, nothing else. The images on your screen, the voice that you hear on your phone, or any other occurrence that looks like magic, gets reduced to zeroes and ones that are eaten by an immensely powerful number-crunching machine the size of your thumbnail.

If you're an attorney, there are things that you just cannot do, such as referring to a law that does not exist or hoping for court procedures that have never been accepted. As a doctor, if the heart stops beating and the blood stops flowing, it would be nonsense to count on the patient to survive without artificial help.

In engineering fields, many things can be done, but going against the laws of physics is just impossible. Furthermore, there are codes and regulations that ensure that risky endeavours, potentially detrimental to the customer, the environment or the public in general, become illegal and are hence avoided most of the time.

But in software-based solutions, there is so much flexibility and power, making the spectrum of workable solutions so diverse that it can become a hindrance instead of an advantage.

Let's take an example: Figure 12 depicts a business objective to transport people and materials from city A to city B. As you can see, there is a slight challenge: a deep roaring river between the two cities. In real life, city planners, engineers and architects would eventually agree that a paved road and a bridge at the location where the chasm is the narrowest is the best option. Then plenty of discussion would follow to decide on materials, type of paving, colors, looks, toll bridge or not, etc. But the main solution wouldn't vary too much.

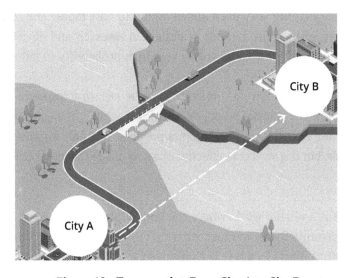

Figure 12 - Transporting From City A to City B

Now, let's transport this objective into the virtual world of information technologies. The potential solutions contemplated could be a paved road and a bridge of course, but other ideas will emerge, such as building a direct tunnel under the chasm, creating heliports in both cities and using an intercity helicopter service, or perhaps employing a giant catapult and a catching device to throw people and materials from one city to the other. The final solution may even be to move city B onto the same bank of the chasm as city A, or to use a teleporter device like in Star Trek.

In the real, tangible world of intercity transportation, there is enough popular knowledge about the laws of physics to simply apply good old common sense. The least costly and safest solution is the road-and-bridge solution. Using helicopters is bound to cost a fortune to operate and isn't very eco-friendly. A catapult looks like a recipe for failure and casualties. A tunnel means digging very deep and is bound to cost more. The teleporter will require billions of dollars in research and development over a few decades with a very high probability of failure.

However, in the virtual world of IT, where electrical impulses are processed by colossal number-crunching machines, the equivalent of these crazy ideas often becomes possible. Not only are they all viable, but the most cost-effective one may not be the most obvious one.

This is a virtual world where the laws of physics as well as the constraints found in most other fields don't apply. It is fair to say that if an IT expert is challenged with a question such as, "Is it doable?" or "Can you make it work?" the answer cannot honestly be "No."

There is always a way to make it work. It may require more effort, more money, more time, more processing power, more data storage, or the newest version of a tool or software, but it will work.

If you have been told "No" by your IT function in the past, let me assure you that apart from extreme cases, the reasons are usually because the budget was exhausted, they could not do it in the allotted time, they had to comply to standards or the teams in place were busy doing other things. It wasn't because it was not doable. There is always a way to make it happen when you're dealing with the intangibles of software and the immense capabilities of computing hardware.

It may just require doing things differently. Unfortunately, doing things *differently* does not always mean finding a totally innovative, out-of-the-box paradigm. Most of the time, it means using the same paradigms and cutting corners.

To illustrate this, here's a question that an IT project manager may ask his team when things start to slip[11]: "... I know that we need to put in more time and effort than we initially planned, but is there a way to make it work and still deliver before the November 1st deadline?"

The IT experts, if put under sufficient pressure, will answer something like, "Hmm, maybe. We could patch this up, make a shortcut here, a bypass there, avoid some controls, write the documentation later, copy the data manually, save a few weeks of work and, maybe, make it for November 1st."

The project manager, who is managing a tight schedule and is also under the spotlight with two schedule and budget delays so far this year, will rejoice in this and make a point of sending congratulatory emails up the hierarchy for the resourcefulness and great spirit of the project team.

---

[11] *I've personally heard that dozens of times, and as a project manager, have done it myself, with these words, or any other variation.*

Does this look like a happy ending? Yes, of course it does, since the project manager, program manager and business sponsors have solved a problem and made possible something that once seemed very much at risk.

In corporate IT more than in any other engineering and design field, anything can be done and made to work. It might be subject to more maintenance, run slower, be less stable, difficult to understand by future employees, need to be replaced sooner, augment costs in other projects or other applications, but it will work. Your IT team works in a world where almost anything can be done and solutions can always be made to work[24]. Hence, for your IT staff to say "No" in all honesty is quite arduous, even when it means cutting corners or using duct tape.

The fact that it fails to conform to the original, approved design or that it's an infringement of corporate quality standards is of lesser importance, especially because the consequences are not that acute. In the virtual world of corporate IT, there is rarely any risk of human injuries or casualties. Thus in my career, I've never seen someone drawn into a court of law for a botched design. External bodies will never audit a project down into its technical details. Events of skimping on quality never get published outside the corporation, and not even outside the project team.

When quality suffers from these shortcuts, the solution will be called a *fix,* a *patch,* or my favorite, a *tactical solution,* to convey recognition that it could have been designed and built in a better way. The worst that can happen is that the quick fixes and shortcuts end up being not so easy to implement after all and the November 1st deadline is missed anyway. What will happen to overall agility in subsequent projects because of this duct-taped solution is often a lesser concern.

Your IT team will find a way to make it work, I can guarantee it. With little effort or heroic tug, and with best practices or haywire, the job will get done. But heroism and best practices require more time and labor. Hence, what looks like a benediction at first sight is indeed one of the causes of the lack of flexibility and agility of the IT platforms in place.

An equally important corollary to remember is this: the fact a solution works is proof of nothing more than it working. Do not even contemplate thinking for a second that it proves anything about the quality of the end product.

You might be tempted to think that if all these virtual things are so flexible, then sub-optimally designed solutions can easily be corrected in subsequent projects. However, I must now bear to you another unpublicized truth about corporate IT and the so-called tactical solutions that you're being told about.

Don't Be Tactically Fooled

Why the So-Called Tactical Solutions Are In Fact Non-Strategic and Permanent Liabilities.

Important clarifications are needed on the *tactical solution* concept introduced above. In IT circles of experienced managers and practitioners, the tactical solution sits somewhere between a fairy-tale and a sham.

The phrase suggests to the non-IT stakeholder that the chosen tactic is on some level a step in the right direction, and that once the subsequent steps are made, we should attain the desired state, often labelled as the *strategic* or *target* solution.

Because the tactical solution works — remember, anything in IT can be made to work — it seems sound to view it as a step in the right direction. After this tactical solution is implemented, we then need to perform the other steps required to attain the strategic state, right?

Not really.

The solution does work and common wisdom says, "If it isn't broke, don't fix it." How could it be broken if it works? Unfortunately, and I know that I am repeating myself, the fact that it works is not a guarantee of anything. Tactical solutions are never presented to you as a step in the wrong direction or a step back, despite being exactly that. And here's the logic.

The next step, after this tactical solution, is not to move forward, but to redo the part of the solution that was sub-optimally designed. The solution will have to be partly dismantled and then redone, throwing away portions of the previous work. That's not a step in the right direction. That's not tactical. That's wasted work.

Not many business people are keen to pay for throwing away something that works, and as such, when money for the next phase becomes available, there is a good chance the sponsor will want to invest into efforts that bring more business value, not rework.

Therefore, for that tactical solution to move toward the strategic goal, the IT team has to hope for luck or fall back on secrecy. They hope to correct the situation in the "lucky" event that the tactical solution eventually breaks or that another major project comes along that allows to openly — or discretely — insert the effort for the needed rework.

Experience has shown me that most of the time, a so-called tactical solution is in reality a permanent solution that sacrifices agility and becomes an IT liability[12] for many years to come.

Now that you know two of the most important truths in corporate IT, let's look at the various sources of unnecessary complexity.

Supernumerary, Extraneous and Unwanted

The Ease At Which Assets Can Be Replicated Creates a Genuine Complexity Issue.

The fact that your organization's IT platforms are made of hundreds of distinct business IT applications is not a problem in itself if the diversity of your business warrants it. Large IT environments consist of a complex web of interacting components, which may just be fine.

But let's be lucid: if you have two accounting packages, three customer relationship management systems, six order processing applications, with your business data copied right and left, and can almost never answer "One, just one!" when asked about the number of systems that support your core processes, then your portfolio of assets has been manufactured by your complexity factory.

---

[12] *The IT Liability idiom is borrowed from the work of Peter Weill & Jeanne Ross from MIT Sloan's Center for Information Systems Research, and refers to the fact that IT investments may create liabilities rather than assets if these so-called assets become a burden in the face of changing business conditions[17]*

The factory piles up disjointed IT solutions, one decision at a time, one project at a time, year after year, to the point where trying to streamline and reduce the footprint becomes a colossal project with very little immediate business value and very little chance to be funded.

I have seen a case for which there were 22 copies of the point-of-sale network. Not by design, but because it seemed quicker and simpler at the time that each copy was made. I have seen a case for which there were 12 copies of the product catalogue. Again, not by design, but because of a lack of communication and skills.

Of course, these are extreme cases. There are also the uncountable cases of data and programs with one or two additional copies. Making copies is so easy and calculating the impact is so ill-supported that these extraneous versions just pile-up over the years until they become unwanted.

The impact of this multiplicity always boils down to time and money. It costs more to keep skilled IT resources knowledgeable in four or five technologies rather than one or two. When a business process changes, modifying six or seven systems costs more than changing just one or two. Running and maintaining 600 applications costs much more than maintaining 100 or 200[13].

And yet, the sheer number of things is not the only issue; their very nature adds substantially to the complexity issue.

---

[13] *If your organization is large enough and old enough, you will easily multiply these figure by 3 or 4 to get to your own numbers.*

Reinventing Wheels
Corporate IT Teams Have An Ill-Controlled Tendency to Recreate Similar Things.

Recreating assets that you already possess usually means duplicating data and functions. In the virtual world of IT, the act of copying stuff doesn't cost much. We can easily talk about triplicating, quadruplicating, and so on, with little extra effort required for the copying. The real price increase comes after. When the time comes to change, enhance, replace or decommission, then you have to duplicate, triplicate or quadruplicate the work hours.

Assuming an average hourly burden rate[14] for IT staff of $100 and efforts counting in days and weeks, it not only uses up valuable money for other projects, but it kills business agility. Even if money is no object, the people that can do the job are scarce resources. Reciprocally, it takes more thinking, better quality processes and stringent design discipline to ensure that systems aren't wrongfully recreated.

The complexity factory is quite productive at creating quasi-similar components that are almost identical to already existing ones with just a little something different that wrongly justifies their existence.

But once created, redundant elements remain difficult to get rid of without investing in their removal, which often means reengineering the solution. Since no sensible business person is keen to undo, remove, redo or reengineer something that works[15], then this new and redundant asset just piles up over your inventory of IT assets.

---

[14] *The total hourly cost of having your own IT staff.*
[15] *Remember, there is always a way to make it work.*

A few years ago, I was part of a team responsible for the development of a billing solution for a telecommunications provider, under the executive sponsorship of the CFO. The packaged application from a reputable vendor had been selected and now was the time to customize and integrate. The team selected to do this was mostly composed of experienced individuals that had been supporting the Finance department's portfolio of applications, along with the vendor's consultants. We were all very excited about this endeavour, which meant the decommissioning of old haywired solutions and replacing them with a brand new asset that would support the envisioned business growth.

The team, including the project manager and the architects, was managed by a senior director responsible for the whole Finance portfolio. I was an outsider, assigned to the project to help the team with the integration portion. The good news is that the project delivered the solution in four phases, with most of the required functionality available in the end. The project was late and over budget, but everyone in the end called it a success.

I am still perplexed about the high rate of declared IT successes for over-schedule and over-budget IT projects, but that's not the issue here. The bad news is that the completed solution was stuffed with data and functions that should have never been part of a billing system. That created several dependencies with other applications, creating the *spaghetti* syndrome, where you cannot touch one part of your platform without impacting the other parts because they are all linked in some way.

My assistance to the team was closer to preaching in the desert than it was to a palatable contribution. There wasn't a week where I didn't have to face a barrage from the whole team regarding the spaghetti thing. Without getting into the technical details, let's just say that an IT pasta meal is never done as a one shot that fills the plate. Entanglement is created one piece at a time, each morsel looking not so consequential. The project team wasn't seeing much evil at copying data locally, because it allowed removing dependencies with other teams.

This silo attitude was incited by the vendor's consultants, who were on a mission to bind the customer (that meant us) to their product. For them, using their product to do any additional function, even those that were already done elsewhere in the portfolio, was a blessing. As a software vendor, the more your product is mingled in your client's critical platforms, the better your business. The vendor-client relationship slowly builds into a tightly bonded marriage where the cost of getting a divorce gets higher with every little piece of misplaced data or function.

The matrimonial binding applied also to the IT team, who was likewise slowly building good internal business. I had very little support in my effort to keep things in the right place and shield them from the spaghetti peril.

This situation is a typical and frequent one in all its flavors and variations. It takes its roots in the presence of several organizational conditions that foster the creation of unwanted complexity. First, the reins where given to one team for all aspects, from requirements gathering to architecture to building the solution to testing and delivering the finished product, even subsequent maintenance and portions of the operation. The billing system was their new baby[16]. The team was not only responsible for too many things, but the judgment of its members about where to place the boundaries around their work was skewed from the onset.

---

[16] *We will dig deeper in IT parenthood in Chapter 2.*

Secondly, the team was exclusively dedicated to one business sponsor — Finance in this case — effectively multiplying the IT silo effect by a line of business (LOB)[17] silo. All debatable technical decisions that were — or should have been — escalated for proper visibility on the long-term impacts rose to a point where the decision makers were Finance-centric. They had little appetite for cross-enterprise sharing of resources of any type.

Thirdly, the processes and discipline required to counterweight the tendency to create detrimental complexity were weak or non-existent. As we will see in the next chapters, the methods that could provide higher-quality solutions are drained by the attribution of decision rights.

Believe me, the simultaneous presence of all these conditions is very commonplace. With no exception whatsoever, I have witnessed this in all the organizations, projects and teams I have worked with, across industries and over time.

Now, repeat this scenario with three or five different teams year after year and you will, sooner than you want, be plagued with three or five tentacular monsters that do everything under the sun, each one performing in its own, slightly different way. Each team will implement portions of functions that are present elsewhere, often without knowledge of their existence.

If all those duplicated components could just stay there untouched forever, that wouldn't be a problem. But business agility means reacting gracefully to change, change and more change. Hence, when a business mutation needs to happen, the number of IT components that must be reopened and modified is multiplied by the number of times wheels were reinvented.

---

[17] *Also dug in Chapter 2 dedicated to IT silos.*

Cross-enterprise agility does not make much of a difference for a siloed IT team, and let's be honest, the more business functions a team puts into its application — its baby — the more indispensable it makes that team.

I have personally witnessed hundreds of occurrences of misplaced data and application functionality, including financial statements outside of finance applications, orders managed outside of the order processing systems, customer files, organizational structure files or points-of-sale definition files replicated in dozens of systems, or a dozen product catalogues outside of product life-cycle management systems.

This is not the result of some carefully crafted conspiracy to extract more money from non-IT businesspeople held hostage by technology. These deviant behaviors are vastly common. Siloed teams and project constraints will encourage IT to respond to a business requirement by using what the team in charge knows best and has direct control over. This is absolutely normal and does not apply only to IT. What's wrong in the case of IT is the absence of healthy processes that help strike a sound balance between team/project agility and business agility at the enterprise level.

This revelation is an important one, but there is more. Even for assets built only once, with no replica, too much customization can also cause big problems.

Customary Custom-Fit

Corporate IT Teams Have a Penchant Toward Customizing Everything.

Let's imagine you are the proud owner of a small urban luxury hotel. The city in question does not really exist and is part of another world where strange things happen, as you will see in a moment. Your hotel has 15 rooms and to make your offer distinctive, every room has been designed and decorated by a different designer.

In one of the rooms, the sink is cracked and you need to replace it, so you call the plumber and schedule him to come the following Monday, as there are no guests in that room for a few days — it's the perfect time to change the defective sink. You've known that it was cracked for quite a while, but had delayed the repair in order get the perfect replacement sink from a fancy special imports boutique. Looks easy enough, but in this parallel world, things aren't always simple.

The washbowl is connected to a cold water pipe, a hot water pipe and a drain — just like in our world — but the cold water pipe is made of wood, the hot water pipe made of copper and the drain is made of cast iron. The diameters of the pipes are respectively five-eighths of an inch, 125 millimeters and three inches. The pressure in the hot water pipe is three times the pressure in the cold water pipe. Now that's not at all like our world.

The following Monday, after 30 minutes spent dismounting the cracked device, the plumber realizes the nature of the pipes and announces the last thing you want to hear: there is a problem. In this world just like in ours, you know this phrase means more time and more money. He explains that the pipes in the wall are custom-made and old, especially the wooden one, since wood tends to rot.

You ask if he could change the old pipes, but he explains that he'd need to make some holes in the walls of this room, the one below and the lobby on the ground floor in order to get to the basement. Thinking about all of these holes and the inconveniences for your fussy guests, you then ask how long these pipes can hold water without leaking. The plumber is unsure. He then advises you that to completely fix the problem, you also need to dig a trench in the front yard, the sidewalk and the street to replace the pipe up to the connector to the city water supply. Unfortunately in your hotel, each and every room has its own set of pipes connected to the street main! With all of this valuable information in hand, you wisely decide not to go that route and keep the wooden pipes for a few more years, hoping for the best.

The friendly plumber then explains that the new sink you purchased — and love — is not compatible with any of the three pipes from the old sink and that you will need custom-made fittings. As you grow paler, the plumber reassuringly tells you not to worry because his brother-in-law owns a respectable machine shop that can do it for a reasonable price. You're hardly reassured, but the plumber then deals what you believe to be the fatal blow: he mentions that there will be a delay of a few days since his brother-in-law is quite busy with other clients at this time. He adds that waiting a few more days shouldn't be a problem since ordering, receiving and installing the high-priced pressure regulator required for the hot water will undoubtedly take a few weeks anyway!

93

As a plumbing story, my fictitious example sounds grossly exaggerated; it is indeed a farce that would not happen in our real world. The plumbing industry benefits from standardized equipment so that when you buy a new sink, there is little chance that it won't fit your existing pipes. And if it doesn't, the hardware store will sell you standard, low-priced adapters.

In the IT world, there are no true cross-industry standards that guarantee compatibility and reduce the need for customization work. Therefore, your IT portfolio is stuffed with nonstandard, custom-fitted components that make every single change more costly. These custom-built components were created over the years because standards were not in place. At times, even when standards existed, they were not always followed for reasons that will become obvious as you read on.

Those with experience in IT integration projects have recognized the similarities between this fictional anecdote and real-life corporate IT. But there is one major difference: in the case of IT, this is the real, day-to-day business. It's not a tale, it's not a joke and it isn't funny.

In real life, no architect, city planner or contractor would be incompetent enough to connect every sink in your hotel to the city's main water pipe under the street. Good practices or just plain old common sense are enough to recognize that only one pipe should be connected to the street's main, distributing water to the rooms from the inside of the building. In the virtual world of IT, things are so flexible that there are numerous ways to get to the same result and make it work. In the virtual world of IT however, common sense isn't always applicable and best practices that should come to the rescue are not always applied.

In real life, a single architect would draw plans for a hotel, followed by the build. Water supply and sewage pipes would then be installed. Each of these things would occur once and be done. But in our fictitious tale, each room was built at different times and different architects were used. Given the virtual nature of IT and computer software, this is commonplace and nothing's wrong with it, per se. You can spend your IT money piece by piece and add new "rooms" to your hotel (new components to your platform); that's fine. What's at fault is that there is no overall blueprint in place to guide the design and the construction of each of the rooms. By managing IT portfolio growth piece by piece, as if all things built before did not exist and as if nothing could be planned in the future, your IT is bound to make wrong design decisions.

In real life, you would not have two technologies for cold and hot pipes. In corporate IT, the equivalent of hot and cold piping may be given to two different individuals, each having its own background and experience, and each deciding to complete the task with the technologies they know best.

In real life, your piping would be standard and compatible with any other sink bought on the marketplace. In standardized industries, you don't have to do anything special; it just happens because that industry has a business model that fosters standardization. As we will discuss further in Chapter 5, your IT team needs to compensate for the absence of cross-industry standards by creating intra-enterprise standards. Unfortunately, there are tar pits and bear traps along the way, unless the right model is put in place.

In real life, you wouldn't be handcuffed to your plumber's brother-in-law for the next 20 years. The sad truth is that for all the things you own in IT that are customized — and most are—you are indeed stuck with the same vendor as long as that asset is around. There is no exit path.

Hence, one of the most productive parts of your complexity factory is related to the noncompliance of solutions to the existing — or non-existing — standards. But there is more. Once a solution is built, probably redundant and surely noncompliant, it sticks around for too long.

Built to Last... Too Long

Corporate IT Teams Are Not Good At Building For Easy Removal.

In many areas other than IT, you would want to build things that last, as the longevity of an asset is usually perceived as a sign of quality. Yet, as with many other things in IT, this is not the case.

Given the pace at which new technology-based business opportunities arise, the ease of replacing solutions is much more valuable than long-lasting solutions. Longevity is mostly viewed as undesirable; it is a vice rather than a virtue in this field.

Business requirements change with time and the components in place, even the well-built ones, will eventually need to be replaced by newer, more powerful technologies. For major rehauls of IT infrastructure[18], the task is not easy, will take time

---

[18] *In IT jargon, this roughly means the physical apparatus (e.g. computers, software, appliances) and the purchased software that runs on it (e.g. operating systems).*

and money, but after two or three years, the servers, desktops and networks will be revamped and ready to last a certain number of years.

Business applications are another story and often turn into a nightmare. These endeavors are usually called *decommissioning* projects. They are so difficult that they frequently take three to five years or more to complete. In many cases, remnants of the old systems are still in place and cannot be removed in an economical way.

I have seen old systems, officially flagged for decommissioning, that remained in function for decades because totally removing them simply cost too much for as a necessary but very low-return investment. I have seen systems built in such a way that removing them required starting a new solution from scratch and resulted in bearing the costs of having two or more systems working in parallel for many years.

In 1990, I was hired by the IT department of a property and casualty insurance company. There was a project to decommission an old policy management system built in the 1970s on technologies invented in the 1960s. The application was a mammoth designed to do everything; it was inflexible and was sandbagging the business. Six years later, I left the insurer and went on to other IT jobs in other industries. In 2012, I came back to work as a consultant with the same insurer that hired me 22 years before. In October of that year, they celebrated the end of the decommissioning of the old policy management system. It took 22 years to get rid of something that was already outdated back in 1990!

Most systems I have dealt with were never built to be dismantled. Nor were they built in order for their constituting parts to be easily replaced by new ones. In many organizations, the end result is somewhere between ludicrous and scandalous: business processes supported by two, three or 10 similar systems, each one just indispensable enough to warrant keeping it alive despite the gross overlap with other assets, the added maintenance costs, and the added burden on new, value-add projects that must take all of that into account.

Hence, we are left with the same question: Why? Why does a whole industry that knows very well that change is the only certainty not create things that are easily removable and replaceable?

The reason is simple: because there are no incentives to do any better. Why would this brand new system be built to be easily dismantled? Isn't it the newest and best thing, with the hottest technologies ever, that is going to propel the business to new heights for years to come? Are you asking your IT team to envision removal of their new baby whereas it is not even born yet?

You might think that acquiring third-party software creates these situations, but again, vendors do not create solutions that are easily dismantled. Not only do they lack incentives for putting in place easy-to-remove solutions, but they truly have hard cash incentives for doing the opposite. They are in business to make money and once the initial sale and implementation are done, yearly maintenance fees kick in. They want to keep earning that money for as long as they can; they have no interest in dismantling their very source of income.

No, IT builders do not think about dismantlement and asking for it would be going against the grain. Moreover, designing and building solutions that are easily removed, or with parts that can be replaced, costs more. This also goes against the grain of managing IT investments one project budget at a time.

But designing for easy pullout is actually very feasible. Some IT architectures are better suited for dismantlement than others. Components can be designed to favor replacement; that is, if there are incentives to do so, of course. Unfortunately, I have never seen or heard of such incentives. The business model in place fosters the opposite.

When it comes to putting in place business solutions, your IT teams are measured on budget and schedule attainment, not on a quality standard that enables these IT components to stand the test of time, including undergoing easy replacement.

Now that you better understand how deeply entrenched the sources of unwanted complexity are, let's take a look at a few excuses often used to soften the crude reality of your much-too-complex IT portfolio.

The Fast Pace of Technologies

The Speed At Which Information Technology Evolves Is Falsely Cited As a Cause For Complexity.

Given the dynamism that characterizes the IT industry and the speed at which technological advances are made, one might conclude that this pace is the main reason for the overwhelming diversity of IT assets in organizations. However, drawing such a conclusion would be easy and superficial, for there is much more behind this.

First, there is the slow evolution of information technologies. Yes, you read that right: *slow*. This might leave you wondering, "What does he mean by slow? Isn't the information technology fast and furiously changing?" Not really. It is actually a slow evolution, as the technology changes that create a real difference and will make your applications obsolete take years before it gets into your operational IT platforms. As excited as we all are today about artificial intelligence (AI) and its potential applications to so many businesses, I should tell you that AI was part of my master's thesis back in 1988.

Do not be fooled by the speed at which new versions of software are thrown at you by vendors. Do not get blinded by a deluge of hype every second year on the newest technology that will change it all — as if the new one would sweep everything else away.

In 1990, I was a young postgraduate that would not touch an outdated technology with a 10-foot pole. Why would I lose time learning something that was already dead and sinking? Or so I thought. Fast-forward to the present and these old technologies are probably running the foundational processes of your business today. Not some peripheral areas, but the core business transactions that provide the daily bread and butter.

Technologies slowly find their way through research centers, whether in innovative, small start-ups or big IT companies. They gradually materialize into immature products and their subsequent versions. They increasingly get adopted through success stories for the brave and horror stories for the brave as well. Articles are written, then books, and years later the technology may be taught in standard IT school curricula.

So yes, new technologies appear on the market, offering possibilities that did not exist before and making the current technologies gradually obsolete. But they do not appear with such speed that your IT team needs to rush it without taking the time to manage the overall complexity.

Adopting a newer technology and planning the obsolescence of an old one should not be mistaken with adding yet another technology on top of your IT asset portfolio. The mere existence of newer technologies does not justify the multiplicity of IT assets that hinder your business agility.
I have worked with so many technology-focused individuals who get excited about the technology itself, simply because it is new, with very little consideration for its true economic value. These IT folks simply want to get their hands on it, just like some people need to have this year's model of car, even if the old one works fine. You must also understand that for many IT professionals, what they can add on their CV can be more important than what is added to the corporate IT landscape.

You want your IT people to be knowledgeable about IT and to be at your organization's forefront for detecting technological opportunities that may lead to a business edge. However, you need proper governance to safeguard yourself from compulsive buyers and put your money where it makes sense. And here's a word of warning: beware of the so-called governance processes in place that control the proliferation of overlapping technologies in your IT basement, for there are formidable silos that are waiting to circumvent these well-intended processes.

The negative side effects of project-oriented IT or the insurmountable impact of ill-defined accountabilities are more efficient at creating complexity than wimpy processes to prevent them.

This leads to holes in the net that allow compulsive buyers free rein and introduce more complexity in your IT portfolio. The so-called fast pace of technologies is not an issue; the distribution of accountabilities is. Those who make the decisions concerning new technologies should be accountable for the global impact of what is introduced, not just the immediate benefit for a given project.

The M&A Myth

Mergers and Acquisitions Create Substantial Complexity, Although Composed of Predictable and Normal Business Changes.

In my career, I have lived through one start-up, three acquisitions (being the acquired one), one de-spin-off (working in a spin-off that went back to the mother company), and a half-dozen acquisitions (acquiring the other company). And that's a pretty smooth ride. I know IT people that were in a continuous fury of acquisitions for 15 years in a row.

For IT teams, mergers or acquisitions are the most cited type of event to justify computing platform complexity. It is often the first that comes to mind in IT circles: "I understand that this is pretty messy, but these systems and that data are inherited from Company ABC prior to merger with Alpha Group" are the kind of answers often heard when asking questions.

And indeed, the mess in question is often easily traced back to some merger endeavor. If your organization has grown through acquisitions, then each takeover, assuming the overtaken company runs a similar business, means inheriting an IT portfolio of about the same complexity as yours. At the very least, you will be doubling your portfolio with each expansion. That is, unless you do something about it. Hence, as part of your merger activities, several projects and programs will be launched to unite the IT assets.

For infrastructure, the IT market is mature enough for you to expect that laptop computers, servers or networks can be merged. You will probably keep the good parts and get rid of the old or useless ones. Without unduly oversimplifying the task — which is far from trivial — your IT team will probably succeed, after a few months to a couple of years of hard work.

For the acquired data, the story is not so simple and regarding the applications, the nightmare has just begun. It may be a decade or more before you see the end of it.

Here is a typical scenario of the costly challenges that your IT team faces when it comes to integrating acquired systems. After a thorough review of the inherited application portfolio, you may decide the gained Customer Relationship Management (CRM) application is much better than the one you had, and consider it as a valuable asset that should be leveraged for the benefit of the entire company. The IT team (also inherited) has the required knowledge and you see a great opportunity to get rid of an old combination of homegrown and half-implemented solutions that your pre-merger CRM was made of. That's sound strategic planning, if not just common sense. Hence, for customer data, you just need to invest in the transfer of all the customer records into the new CRM and decommission the old stuff, right? Well, not exactly.

Transferring the data will not be a walk in the park, because from the outset, it just doesn't fit into the new customer management application. It is almost a certainty that the overtaken business applications use a slightly different vocabulary.

I used the word *slightly* on purpose, to make you believe for a second that a slight difference could be solved by investing slightly more time and money. But that's not the way it works. Information systems and technologies suffer from a fundamental weakness. Despite their great powers, they do not tolerate ambiguity. In the end, everything being stored with ones and zeros, "F" for female gender and "W" for woman, is not the same. If you push the former into the latter, it will break and crash. And system crashes as we saw in Chapter 3 are measured and have high impact on IT careers.

This will make it difficult to merge the data without first involving a team of IT professionals to convert the customer records. What you do for CRM needs to be repeated for production line systems, inventory management, finance packages, order processing, legal, HR and the whole set of newly acquired applications.

Complexity is sometimes such an issue that, out of urgency or because of the sheer cost of the task to complete the data migration, some organizations will decide to keep running applications that they should have decommissioned.

Now, if you repeat this scenario for a dozen applications, you may end up keeping more applications and databases that add up to your pre-merger platforms. Repeat this again for five or 10 acquisitions, and you have a genuine pile of overlapping and quasi-identical business applications to maintain.

We haven't even touched on the cases of human pushback in the operational trenches or cultural clashes between the pre- and post-merger teams that will also impact the IT work required to rationalize the IT portfolio.

Instead of the daunting task of streamlining by eliminating the duplicate business applications, your IT team may decide to keep them and "integrate." After all, if it's too costly to get rid of the unwanted applications, at least they could make them talk to one-another in a harmonious cohabitation. If in the end, the processes run in all areas, important business data is safely transferred to financial systems and the merger appears grace-fully on the corporate financial statements, the shareholders and auditors should have the warm feeling that this move has created one bigger, stronger and united entity.

But again, for the integration, IT teams will face the same challenge as with the merging of business data: disjointed vocabularies between applications that need to interact and an incompatible interface[19]. The underlying IT architectures of collaborating business applications will be so different that other highly-skilled IT experts will be needed to find a way to bridge the gaps with what we call "the glue code"[20] that makes this giant collage work.

---

[19] *The equivalent of the pipe fittings in your boutique hotel.*

[20] *Used to categorize portions of computer programs whose sole purpose is to connect parts that are technically incompatible. The potential reasons for incompatibility are numerous.*

Don't be misled, for the glue that makes this work may very well be tons of concrete poured over your IT assets, making them harder to own, costly to maintain or tough to dismantle, forever after.

So yes, in a way, the why and wherefore of complexity, rationalized to the miseries of M&A, is not untrue at all. But putting all the blame on mergers and acquisitions is an easy way out and a fallacious one at that.

After all, an acquisition or a merger is a business change. A drastic and painful one maybe, but nevertheless a business change that involves new customers, new employees, a new organizational chart, new markets, new products, new distribution channels, new brands, new assembly lines, new buildings, new production means, etc. Isn't that normal business change? Concentrated maybe, on steroids perhaps, but business change still. What is so strange, exceptional or extraordinary about all of the above changes? Shouldn't you expect that your IT team put in place solutions that can handle variations like new product lines, new territories or new customers?

Indeed, you should. Well-built IT components should be able to sustain each and every one of these changes elegantly, without huge projects that last for years and without having to admit failure for not getting rid of inextricable IT components.

Mergers and acquisitions are not a cause for the multiplication of similar IT components. The true reason is the inability of the existing or acquired assets to sustain business changes. It's a quality issue. I recently had a discussion with an executive from a North American agri-food company on the challenges of M&A. This senior manager explained that his corporation has grown mainly from acquiring smaller businesses at the rate of two per year for the last half-century. Despite the fact that this is an obvious pattern, repeated steadily over decades, he sadly reminded me that the financial systems and data of the firms acquired during the last seven years have not yet been integrated. I didn't dare to ask how many, but figured that their internal IT function had a backlog of 14 acquisitions to complete. That's a lot. Neither did I dare tell him that accounting and finance systems are perhaps the most standardized across all industries. I felt somewhat ashamed of the business I am in [21].

So the fundamental question is why existing IT assets, and especially data and applications, aren't more flexible in the face of change? The blunt answer is that they most likely haven't been designed and built to sustain much change. And the fundamental reason for the inability of IT teams to create platforms with the right virtues is not lack of technical knowledge; it is related to conflicting accountabilities and unbalanced distribution of decision rights about how assets should be built.

But there is more. Let's now look at the two big factors that cause IT teams to throw all good intentions out the door in order to satisfy short-term priorities.

---

[21] In a 2006 survey of 420 corporate executives, Accenture reported[54] that only 30% of respondents claimed successful IT integration I their latest cross-border M&A deal, which concur with my personal field observations.

Budget and Urgency

Resource or Schedule Issues Are Over-Abused Justifications For Short-Sighted Decisions That Spread Unnecessary Complexity.

An over-exploited reason to account for the growing complexity of business application portfolios is a lack of time or money to perform the necessary changes to fix it. I cannot count the number of times when, in the face of a more than questionable architectural choice, the reason invoked for decree was "No more time" or "Not enough money." Nothing new here. In all areas of business, and I'd say in all areas of life in general, there comes a time where there is a shortage of resources, the most common and universal ones being time or money.

In many other areas than IT, with less time and less money, you usually get less, period. In a construction project, if the sponsor runs out of money, something will certainly be missing. A wing of the building will be left with just foundations and nothing above. Rooms or entire floors will be left unfinished — and uninhabitable. But rarely will the sponsor get the same benefits — same usable space, same lighting, same window size — for less money. Quality specifications can be lowered, but usually, it will show and the customer will notice the difference. So if doors are hollow, if the building is badly insulated, if flooring is on the cheap side, the owner will not get the same benefits. Since the construction industry is standards-based, and especially enforced for buildings of a certain size or commercial use, there are things that will never be done by a contractor to lower costs for fear of the consequences of noncompliance to local codes. If a contractor dared to, let's say pour six-inch-thick basement concrete walls where the minimum requirement is 12, he'd be looking at such trouble that he'd simply never do it.

With IT-based business solutions, as we saw in Chapter 4, there is always a way to make things work. Worse, many of the options to make things work for less money or time look about the same from the outside. Very often, the shoddy stuff is hidden under the hood. Supplement this with the customer who doesn't even know how to lift that hood, let alone ascertain the quality of the mechanics. Add also, as we will see in Chapter 5, that quality is in many areas undefined and uncontrolled. Hence, budget and urgency become even more compelling arguments for cutting corners.

I cannot count the number of times these projects ended up over schedule or delayed, despite the quick fixes. Nor can I count the number of times these over-scheduled projects would have managed, if given enough time, to design and build the solution properly anyway. From a budget perspective, these projects were part of a bigger program that ended up, over the next few years, spending tens of millions of dollars and for which that single project's budget increase for the right solution was in the end just a drop in the ocean anyway. Too often, wrong design decisions were made because of project budget or schedule constraints and they were never properly communicated to the business sponsor who not only provided the funding, but now has to live with the consequences for the years to come.

Budget constraints and urgency are not the true reasons behind your overly complex and inflexible IT portfolio: short-sighted technical decisions are at fault.

You may be tempted to think that over-complexity is just a quality-related issue that is technical in nature and should be dealt with by technical people. But because of the way roles are distributed in IT, nobody's really accountable for the negative effects of redundant, over-customized or low-quality, corner-cut solutions. These solutions become genuine permanent work products that you're stuck with for years that often turn into decades.

Your IT management and staff know very well that additional complexity makes the organization's portfolio heavier to own and maintain, and ultimately hinders responsiveness to business change. So why are they letting teams get away with such decisions?

I will describe in more detail in the next chapter how project orientation and other silos help to justify implementing myopic technical solutions. But before we dive into these silos, there is one crucial element in the equation that you must be aware of: building for flexibility and agility usually cost more and does so right from the outset.

The Flip Side of Agility

There Is No Free Lunch: Containing Complexity and Building For Agility Takes More Time.

Experience in the implementation of IT business solutions is invaluable because it allows you to be confronted, repeatedly, with situations where it is obvious that if the existing system had been architected differently, it would have made things simpler. There are ways to design IT systems that either hinder or foster flexibility, but there is no magic and no free lunch, even in the virtual world of information technologies. Building your IT platforms for business agility and quick turnaround times comes with a major drawback: generally speaking, creating an IT asset that is flexible costs more up-front.

In all possible scenarios, architecting and designing a flexible solution will take more time. The rationale is quite simple: in order for your solution to be more flexible in the face of time, you have to think about the future, define potential scenarios, apply experienced creativity, draw parallels and investigate uncovered areas. In short, you have to take more time to define a smart solution. You cannot just rely on being smarter — although that won't hurt.

In addition to design, the amount of work required to build a system with embedded adaptability may be equivalent, and in most cases, somewhat longer.

So there is no way to escape this: building smart, flexible and resilient solutions takes more time. To help you understand why flexibility costs more, here's a fictitious example from beyond the IT world.

Suppose you have to design a truck, and the requirements are:

> *Capacity to transport, on paved roads, raw material up to 10 tons and the ability to dump.*

You'd probably design a 10-wheeler dumpster. Now, suppose we changed the requirements to the following:

> *Capacity to transport on paved roads various construction apparatus, or raw materials up to 20 tons, or liquid petroleum products, and the ability to dump raw materials.*

In the second case, you would need three different trucks because raw materials require a dumpster body, construction materials require a flatbed and liquid petroleum requires a tanker.

But the requirement says one truck, not three. And if you're smart and seeking flexibility through reuse, you would design a semi-trailer solution with a single tractor and three trailers adapted to the payload. It will take more time and skills to design this smart and flexible solution. Each trailer will need to be attached to the trailer, requiring a hitch mechanism. Each trailer will need a separate chassis, as well as the tractor. The tractor and trailers will need special connectors and flexible cables for electricity and hydraulics. Each trailer will require a stand device to keep it level when there is no tractor to support it. Each trailer will require a separate licence plate and governmental fillings and permits.

A project would deliver them in several steps. In phase one, it would be the tractor and the dumpster trailer, and it would cost more than just the 10-wheeler design. Phases two and three would deliver the other trailers, at a lower unit cost than two separate trucks. On the longer term, the one tractor and three separate trailers solution will cost less to acquire and less to operate than three distinct trucks[22]. In the end, it takes more time to design and build, with the promise that subsequent phases will cost less.

The truck metaphor has its limits, however. In IT, you have to design everything, but in the trucking world you can simply buy a 10-wheeler. When the project changes scope, you can subsequently sell it on the used trucks market and buy a tractor and all the trailers you need.

---

[22] *With a few assumptions about how you will operate of course.*

Corporate IT is becoming more standardized, especially in the infrastructure sub-domain, but it will take time — lots of time — before your business applications can be replaced with such ease.

Meanwhile, the assets you get, you keep. You won't sell them on the used market and buy a replacement just like that. IT solutions and systems are hard to dismantle and replace. And this is mostly due to lack of vision in the design.

Convincing a business sponsor to invest more money to get exactly the same tangible results in the first phase, with the promise that subsequent costs will be reduced or that future project delivery times will be shortened, is more than a challenge. It's a campaign with disproportionately poor weaponry against the short-term benefits enemy.

As you will read in the next chapter, there are formidable silos built around teams and processes that feed the creation of re-invented, redundant or cemented IT assets.

CHAPTER FOUR TAKEAWAYS

- *Computers and software are so flexible and powerful, that in corporate IT, anything can be made to work, one way or another.*

- *A solution that works is by no means a sign of its quality.*

- *So-called tactical solutions need to be thrown away and redone to make them strategically aligned.*

- *Complexity is spawned in your IT assets with: (1) multiplication of data; (2) reinvention of analogous components; (3) over-customization; and (4) creation of hard-to-remove pieces.*

- *Complexity is often blamed on (a) the speed of change of information technologies; (b) mergers and acquisitions; or (c) urgency. But these are fallacious exits to toss away the real issues.*

- *Building IT assets for flexibility, speed and agility takes more thinking, time and effort.*

- *A new distribution of roles can transmute corporate IT to an organization that continuously improves its ability to deliver high-quality outputs.*

5. SILO WARS

How Corporate IT Silos Undermine Quality and Exacerbate Complexity

Anyone with experience in organizations of a certain size has seen the adverse effects on performance when people do not talk to one another or when teams are not properly coordinated. Corporate IT is no different and does not escape the natural tendency for individuals and groups to shield themselves from external factors in order to stay focused on their objectives. In the next pages, we will go through three types of silos[25] that are surely present in your IT function. You will gain insight into the effect they have on the quality of IT work and the systematic creation of complexity. First, we'll look at the silos created by IT investment budgets that are divided into lines of business. Then, we'll delve into the silos that teams create within IT, and finally, we'll discover how the project-orientation of IT leads to an underestimated source of vacuum work.

LOB Silos

The Allocation of IT Budgets Can Create
Line-of-Business Silos That Are Hard to Cut Through.

Take, for instance, a project that has to deliver a new order management system for a telecommunications company, sponsored by the residential products LOB. The residential division, headed by a senior VP, needs to revamp the system in order to provide more self-service options from the web and mobile apps, and the upgrade must integrate with the new network fulfilment software that the engineering division has purchased. The goal is to reduce the time to activate certain services (cable, fixed lines, home security, etc.), thus improving the customer journey.

In the telco industry, residential services are mass products where customization is limited in order to present simple offers and competitive costs. Residential products are designed with a cookie-cutter philosophy, where all customers are deemed to have similar requirements and no customization is done, other than pre-defined parametrization (such as choosing channels or certain pre-defined option kits).

On the other hand, telco's commercial LOB that takes care of business customers has the opposite philosophy. They will bend over backwards to satisfy a commercial customer, digging trenches and deploying miles of new fiber optic cable to give them what they want. It's a stark contrast to the residential division, where if a service is not available in a given location, the customer is simply out of luck.

At a higher level, the business processes that support order management in the two LOBs are quite different. I should also mention that the customer demographics and profit margins are diametrically opposed: on one hand, you have low-profit, standardized services sold to millions of clients, and on the other hand, highly-customized services sold to fewer, but more lucrative accounts.

It's important to note that some commercial customers will use residential components of a telco's network. For example, a pizza delivery chain may require sophisticated services for its headquarters, but simple cable service for its pizza outlets that use the same network services as residential customers. Hence, although the commercial and residential LOB have fundamental differences, they can also overlap.

Now, let's get back to our example. One of the IT architects assigned to the project suggests a design that fulfills the immediate requirements for the residential LOB, but uses a more standard design that will make some of the sub-processes — such as the simple cable service activation — available to any other processes in the future[23].

As such, the current project would deliver components that could eventually support the commercial LOB when they start revamping their order processing application in 18 months. By using a flexible design, the residential-only solution paves the way to more change resilience for the whole telco, as the proposed architecture allows for better reuse and adaptability to new business processes that are bound to appear.

This is an example of basic architecture wisdom that represents a step in the right direction toward building more flexible appli-

---

[23] *Without getting technical, let's just point out that the suggested path is to carefully design the solution to make portions of the result applicable to other lines of business or other contexts.*

cation platforms. But the wisdom stops here, for there are many roadblocks ahead.

There is a premium to pay for building flexible IT business solutions. In most cases, the extra cost resides in the effort required to analyze the bigger business issues, identify the commonalities, perform reviews and quality control processes, and in the end, design the solution the right way.

Flexible solutions take a mix of technical knowledge, art, experience, and — most of all — vision above and beyond the stated requirement. Unfortunately, relying on this wisdom and vision can also be interpreted, especially by the project manager, as an open bar for unplanned scope. For a project manager, this is pure evil.

For obvious reasons, budgets allocated for a given line of business are for the sole use of that line of business. If the IT Investment Committee decides the residential LOB will get funding to revamp its order entry this year and for the next three years, and the commercial LOB must put part of their investments into CRM and prospect management, these decisions must be adhered to.

But back to our IT architect with the forward-thinking idea. The residential business sponsor will immediately ask the IT architect if this flexible design is strictly required to fulfill its LOB requirements, as well as if there's a premium for building the solution that way. The answers to these two questions are: No, it is not technically a requirement for *that* LOB, and yes, it will add costs to *that* project.

If we stop for a moment and elevate ourselves above project budgets and lines of business, we know that all these requirements will need to be fulfilled at some point. We also are pretty confident that in the end, it will cost more to do things twice. But when your vision and all your senses are funnelled into mundane project management logic or immediate business benefits, as you can expect, the yes and no answers are a major roadblock. The senior executive responsible for this project or program budget has committed, not only to invest in IT, but most importantly to achieve business results through a well thought-out business case. Most likely, the business case does not include business results from any other LOB.

When these types of design options are raised, there is usually no easy mechanism to go beyond the silo effect of investment budgets and LOB imperatives to validate if the design opportunity could indeed be a valid business opportunity.

In the telecom example above, it's possible that the commercial line of business would have been interested in comparing the cost delta between building a flexible and reusable solution for their evolving needs today versus waiting for a year or two to build the same thing. If the economics are compelling, business executives might conclude that seeding some money to compensate for the cost delta today would be better for the commercial LOB.

Unfortunately, I have never seen, read or heard of an easy process for submitting such opportunities to those in charge of managing the investments and their expected returns.

Most investment governance processes empower the business decision-makers to influence *where* IT investments will be spent in order to align them with business strategies. But *how* solutions should be built is rightfully not on the agenda of this type of committee.

Unless this funding is part of a bigger, cross-enterprise program that spans all lines of business, chances are the sponsor has no immediate interest in adding to the scope of the investment for the benefit of other lines of business. In other words, the sponsor is measured on the effectiveness of this investment by the bottom line of her LOB. Helping other LOBs, teams or divisions is fine and noble, as long as there is no foreign hand in the wallet, no risk on delivery dates and no impact on expected results.

Line of business and investment budget allocations are strong contributing factors to the creation of silos. However, there is another culprit at work here: the way your IT function is organized adds yet another layer to the silo effect.

IT Silos

The Organizational Structure of the IT Function Creates Strongholds of Complexity-Generating Vacuum Effect.

The IT organizational structure may also be modeled to lines of business. As such, the IT teams and their managers are assigned — loosely or strictly — to specific lines of business to support finite portfolios of business applications. We saw in Chapter 4 that unwanted complexity is often fueled by design decisions made in a vacuum.

Each business application in your portfolio of assets has been created or put in place by a team that now maintains and enhances it. The size of these teams can range from one or two experts to a whole floor of busy folks. Regardless of the magnitude of the team, they probably view the IT application they are supporting as their baby.

Like any other baby, it entails attachment as well as a skewed opinion about the value of the asset, its place in the corporate landscape and the evolution path the asset should go through.

Add to this the fact that this application or set of applications also represents their bread and butter, and these experts are bound to have strong gut reactions to certain questions. If you ask them "How can you reduce the amount of work required to maintain the application?" or "How could we decommission this application and merge the data onto another application to reduce complexity and save time and money?", the first answers you will get are litanies of apparently insurmountable technical reasons for not doing it or warnings that it would be a very costly endeavor if you ever dared to do such a foolish thing.

Asking individuals who work in these teams to even consider giving up their baby after years of devoted pampering goes against the grain of professional engagement, job satisfaction and a sense of belonging to your organization.

Worse, they are probably the only ones technically capable of slaughtering the infant, since no one can, for all sorts of good and bad reasons, just unplug the thing. You need (once again) IT experts to remove it. With technological know-how being the foundation of their expert status, the expert's perception of their own usefulness within your organization will be shaken once their application is gone. Hence, you can expect resistance to streamlining the portfolio or building components that span across the organization.

Here, too, asking IT to build assets that support multiple lines of business goes against the grain of the IT organization itself, with more resistance in sight on the part of the IT managers and teams that need to build the solution. In any case, all sorts of reasons to avoid collaborative efforts will emerge.

I have seen many variations of this resistance at work, ranging from open refusal, to discrete sabotage through information hiding, as well as physical absence, parallel agendas, open non-collaboration, or my favorite, raising the specter of some abominable ending. Forcing a team or its direct line of management to make difficult decisions that in many cases will result in staff reductions is doomed to failure.

Without revisiting the distribution of decision rights regarding the destiny of applications and technologies, these silos will slow down any streamlining endeavor, and as such, perpetuate unnecessary complexity.

There is one last shadow on the silo skyline that we must explore, comprised of a set of mandatory and highly praised processes for delivering IT solutions: project management.

Project-Oriented IT
Each IT Project Is a Silo Where Project Management Logic Is Ruthlessly Applied and Detrimental to the Quality of Your Platforms.

Every organization has a process for determining how much money, and on which endeavors, should be spent in IT. Once the investment decisions are reached, the funds required to achieve the desired strategies are attached to projects and programs.

In project-oriented IT, the project is the fundamental conduit through which changes materialize. In all cases and variations of the IT investment mechanics, the project becomes the legal tender of IT change (Figure 13).

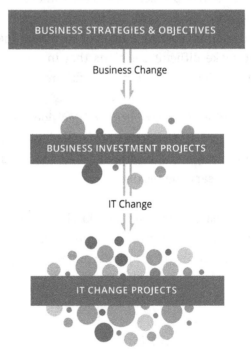

Figure 13 - Projects, Legal Tender for IT Change

The executives who have carefully chosen the investment strategies, selected the best projects to achieve these, and allocated funds from a limited pool of financial resources, provide a clear mandate to the project manager (the PM).

As a project management professional certified by the Project Management Institute (PMI)[27], let me assure you that seasoned project managers (PMs) are very well acquainted with the obligations that come with cost management[26]. Monthly statuses to sponsors that include budget consumption, pressure from the project management office (PMO) to provide weekly numbers for global reporting, budget forecasting, earned value calculation, and much more, are institutionalized reminders that corporate money in the custody of the PM must be scrupulously managed.

In every organization, there is a process known as the "Project Change Management Process." It has some visibility up in the hierarchy and you must therefore be convincing.

For all the projects that I managed, having to ask for more time or money was never a walk in the park. The mere existence of the project change management process might give the impression that the organization is willing to allow changes in projects, but that is far from being the case. Even the most insensitive PM can feel, from all stakeholders, that a change order is never really welcomed. The reasons for this are simple. First, the budget is set and was allocated last year, from the highest governance instances. Second, IT has promised something, at a given cost, for a given date, but is now telling the customer that it's not the case anymore. No customer, whatever the field, likes to be told that the budget set aside will not suffice. Thirdly, the reasons are often obscure or just plain technical, leading the sponsor to adopt a position where he or she is simply expecting IT to find a way to complete the project within the agreed parameters.

Regardless of the PM's talent or the probity of the request, the fact remains that the PM is asking for a change in budget or schedule, which is always frowned upon.

Project Managers have another important responsibility, risk management. The PMs' job to mitigate risk means that she must identify anything that can go wrong, evaluate it and do something about it before a problem occurs.

As such, seasoned project managers have developed a sixth sense for the detection of potential risks. It sits somewhere between intuitive awareness and experienced paranoia. Going to bat for a schedule extension or more money is not an easy task, therefore, anything that may go wrong and get in the way of project success must be avoided until proven otherwise.

One of the most common risks in IT project management is what has been called *scope creep*. In my experience, scope creep is rooted in two types of situations: oversights or the *why not* syndrome. The first is quite obvious to imagine. Inexperience, lack of skills, deficient estimation techniques, insufficient planning or just the fact that your IT operating platform is a humongous and unmanageable monster, can lead to the high probability of missing something.

The second is more subtle. It comes from the tendency of stakeholders to pack as much as possible into a given project because they know that the opportunity is now. Let's take a common building renovation example: the project scope is to renovate the kitchen. The plan is to remove a portion of a wall to create a more open space. However, when the interior wall is removed, you realize that at the junction with the exterior wall, the insulation dates pre-WW2. A decision is made to strip the wall and re-insulate before the new cabinets are installed. Was this budgeted for? Of course not; that's why it is called scope creep. The same could be said for the electrical wires that aren't up to code. If it's not in the budget, it's scope creep. Then there is the case of your spouse realizing that a heated floor would be sooo much more comfy and could be done before the new ceramic tiles are glued into place. Again, if it's not planned for, it's scope creep.

For a project manager, all of this creepy stuff is poison. Whatever the reason, whatever the benefit, the only certainty is that it will inflate, not maximize, time and cost investment. The PMs and the project management processes around them are key safeguards against schedule slippage and cost overrun, such as scope creep and many other areas where things can go wrong.

If organizations want to successfully tackle IT change, they must enforce the systematic use of a sound project management practice. However, managing all IT change through project management practices only, without proper counterbalancing mechanisms, has major drawbacks.

We now need to throw in a few typical examples where the organization's greater good is sacrificed for adherence to strict project management practices.

An IT architect working on the solution design of one of several projects may — and this is desirable behavior for an architect — identify that other projects have similar requirements, and suggest that a single component be created for all projects rather than being repeated separately.

Common wisdom suggests that having only one component will cost less in the execution of all projects and should cost less over the years to support and maintain. But things are not that simple in project-oriented IT.

There is always an immediate roadblock for the architect who designs a component to be reusable: the project manager. The PM is engaged in her project, not other projects, and has limited visibility on overall investment strategies.

The first line of defence on real or perceived scope creep is the project manager, who has a very sharp eye for detecting anything that may increase cost, time or risk aspects of her projects.

Designing for flexibility costs more; that's a given. The benefits come later, most of the time in subsequent projects. If the PM already has a previously completed cost estimate in hand, she will ask if this design was assumed in the original evaluation. If no evaluation has been done yet, then she will ask if this flexible design will cost more than doing it without consideration for other projects, LOBs, IT assets, etc. The answer to these questions, in all honesty, will be: No, it was not part of the original estimation assumptions and yes it will cost more.

The IT architect attempting to convince a PM about the costs savings of a more flexible asset is defeated from the start. Without hard numbers on the net effect on IT productivity, maintenance staff or future delivery schedules, the battle is lost.

We're back to the same type of roadblock depicted in the previous chapter, except that this time we are much further away from the business decision-maker, hence further away from the broader view. Business sponsors and executives are rarely involved in these mundane discussions and investment strategies or economies of scale are never on a PM's radar.

One thing is sure: the immediate answer of any PM officially responsible for project budget, and the hassles associated with asking for more time or money, will be "No."

The net effect of this answer is that the project's risks will be contained, but the quality of the asset will be degraded.

Project-oriented IT management is a silo that inhibits viewing assets as cross-enterprise resources. Worse, it forbids viewing IT assets together: everything is a project, and it has a budget. Having in place a defined set of quality standards and effective processes to check for compliance is the only way to reduce or eliminate these behaviors.

The problem is that the usual corporate IT engagement model does not support it. Worse, it indirectly encourages siloed behaviors. The design, construction and quality checks needed to deliver a solution are under one single umbrella that is evaluated for on-time and on-budget delivery above everything else. The allocation of IT investment money per LOB and the assignment of projects exclusively to each LOB just add another layer of hindrance to the management of true IT assets and their quality levels. Project-oriented IT creates an even more fertile soil for IT complexity to grow.

And Then, Unplanned Things Happen

When Things Go Awry in Corporate IT, Quality Becomes Secondary To Short-Term Performance Measures.

It would be overoptimistic to believe that silos could be avoided by silo-cutting processes to prevent the isolation of teams. In fact, the way accountabilities are distributed or performance is measured creates deeply rooted behaviors that support silos. Especially when the unforeseen arises.

A few years back, I was involved in an IT project that would deliver a network trouble management application to field technicians in the telecommunications industry. The project was more than halfway through its three-phased schedule, but was experiencing budget and calendar issues. The problem was typical, but nevertheless real: the requirements used when the project was originally planned and funded were only partially identified and an entire section of the business processes had been missed.

As the project team started to dig, it became obvious that more time and effort would be required. The issue was brought up to the project sponsor in order to secure more funds, but unfortunately there was a freeze on spending. The sponsor had no leeway, but without this added work, the project's business value was jeopardized. It didn't make any sense to deliver something with that part missing.

The project manager came back to the project team with a mandate to find ways to make the project fit within the budget, but nonetheless bring something valuable for the phase one delivery date, planned for the fourth quarter.

Several options were examined, including cutting back on functionality, on targeted groups of field technicians, on reporting and on data integration with other systems. Unfortunately, the planned scope for phase one was already bare-bones. The team was left clueless until someone made an observation about conformance with some of the corporate IT quality standards. By skipping some of those standards requirements, the project could save some effort, without jeopardizing immediate business value or schedule.

The corporate quality standards stated that all new applications had to feed operational information to a central component intended to provision the data warehouse. But the data warehouse was already fed by an older, less flexible mechanism that could be kept alive without disrupting current processes. The data warehouse's main users were Finance and Marketing. This requirement did not provide immediate value to the project sponsor who could get reports directly out of the system, and who saw this requirement as technical rather than a business one.

Of course the architects — including myself — manifested their disapproval. The main argument was that by not complying with the standards, the resulting asset would be harder to integrate with other applications and systems when phases three and four came about. Essentially, it would take more time and money at a later date to undo the shortcut and redo it the right way.

But the project manager reminded us that all other alternatives had been exhausted and without this shortcut he would have to go back to the sponsor and admit the team's failure to find a solution. The team knew that such a conclusion would probably mean the end of the project until further notice.

Remember that everyone's job on the team directly depended on project activities. The architects silently surrendered to pressure from their colleagues.

The decision was carefully documented and communicated to show the utmost importance for the business to have the new system in place and the stringent economic realities that the corporation was facing. The project presented a dispensation request to the architecture review board[24], with a clear declaration that this solution was *tactical* and that further phases of the program would make the system compliant to the agreed-upon standards.

When that issue arose, it was not presented back to the IT Investment Committee[25] to show the new ROI figures (or any other metric used). For there was no one with any genuine interest in doing this, since all the involved stakeholders were directly involved in the project. From the IT trenches up to the business sponsor, everyone wanted this project to complete by the planned date.

Hence, the business case originally presented as a basis for justifying the investment was not readjusted. Had it been presented to a neutral and detached body to reassess the value, would it have been canned or would it have simply been allocated more

---

[24] *We will get into more details about the Architecture Review Board (ARB) in Chapter 5.*

[25] *This is a common label for an executive committee that is responsible for the allocation of IT funds, and for the governance of how the money is spent and the expected business benefits. We shall get into more interesting details in Chapter 5.*

money based on more than sufficient return ratios? Nobody knows. Impact analysis of project decisions that affect IT assets for years to come is almost always made in a project vacuum. Not knowing about the impact of project decisions outside a given project is one factor. But there is something else: an established pattern that fosters little knowledge about past projects and an unwillingness to know more.

Institutionalized Amnesia

In Corporate IT, No One Ever Remembers Why Platforms Are in Such a State of Complexity.

A project being, by definition, a temporary endeavor, it has a start and a finish date. What happens before kickoff or after the project concludes is simply not part of the equation. At the closure of the project, the team is dismantled and every one moves onto other things. The show stops there.

As you will see in Chapter 5, the quality of what is delivered is secondary to on-time delivery of the project. If what is created works, the project will move on.

The systematic creation of unnecessary complexity by IT projects has absolutely no impact on the project that creates it. The impact is felt on future projects, most of which are not yet started. That's why project-oriented IT will systematically favor design and architecture options where benefits are foreseeable within the project. Anything that may or will happen after a project completion date is accessory. Project orientation, aimed at short-term objectives, will neglect several aspects of quality and continuously produce IT components that are more complex than they should be. And since IT assets' qualities, including complexity, are not quantitatively measured, then preventing the perpetual creation of convoluted solutions is a lost battle against short-term, quantified project performance objectives.

In the early stages of a project, plenty of effort is put into estimating the work that has to be done within that project. In project-oriented IT, there is no point evaluating the work done prior to that project: anything that happens prior to its start date is not within its scope. When a project starts, the only important elements are the current state of things, the project objectives and the resources available. If the current state of the IT assets are a total mess, no one has the time or the interest to go witch hunting on past projects. Clocks are reset — as it should be — but organizational memory is also flush during reboot.

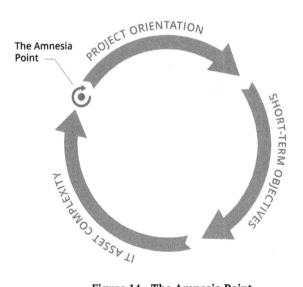

Figure 14 - The Amnesia Point

And the circle goes on and on, project after project, amnesia after amnesia, year after year, until a point when even those that know how messy your IT assets are — and why — can only shrug their shoulders and sigh. The only way to stop this vicious circle of IT memory blackouts is to make someone accountable for the overall state of things, not just for the individual projects that created it. There is no other way. The blind spot in the area of accountabilities must be eliminated.

Fighting against silos is a never-ending war. When you succeed to cross silos, don't lower your guard for a second; they will come back. There is nothing special about portions of large organizations wanting, and in the end succeeding, at reducing process complexity by working in a vacuum. It exists in all fields and always has. However, IT's case is unique because the mechanisms to counterweight and contain excessive vacuum work are weak at best.

Standardization, quality controls, enterprise architecture and asset management are all known instruments that could — and should — come to the rescue. But as we will see in the following chapter, the issue of roles render these instruments helpless, causing your IT assets to suffer from siloed teams and unnecessary complexity.

CHAPTER FIVE TAKEAWAYS

- *The first silo is the way investment money is allocated, usually by line of business, impeding the creation of shared assets.*

- *The second set of silos originates from corporate IT's organizational structure. It also impedes sharing and additionally hinders streamlining of IT assets.*

- *The third set of silos is composed of dozens to hundreds of discrete projects that deter the sound management of IT assets.*

- *When problem arise, all stakeholders retreat to their respective silos.*

- *Corporate IT is afflicted with severe amnesia when it comes to why the portfolio of assets is filled with over-complex and poor-quality components.*

- *Better designed distribution of accountabilities would help cut through silos, raise quality and reduce complexity creation.*

6. ASSET QUALITY

How Roles Issues Affect Asset Management, Quality, Projects and Agility

Conflicting roles are the guilty source of so many pains. Complexity is the monster on the lookout. Silos are the fortresses that perpetuate all of this. But in the end, the quality of your dearly paid assets is what's it's all about.

In this chapter you will discover that even though the solutions that IT builds[26] for you might work, they are rarely treated as assets at all. The problem begins with how they are documented.

---

[26] *Keep in mind that assets hereby refer to business solutions mostly made of software. The management of the infrastructure portion of your IT is, without hesitation, the closest to genuine asset management.*

Truant Documents for Legacy

Documentation Is Created To Attain Measured Performance Objectives, Not To Enhance Asset Quality.

In the old house I bought, something bugs me on an almost daily basis: there is a window missing in my living room. It would make a world of difference if there was an additional opening on one of the walls. The whole room is crying for that window. If I call a contractor to get a price, he will give me a quotation established on an analysis of the situation, based on facts and assumptions. Facts that can be observed and assumptions about non-visible characteristics of a house built in the 1940s in that neighborhood.

Now what if the contractor had absolutely no idea about what is inside that wall? That's pretty simple: I would never get a real fixed-price bid. The answer I would receive is an hourly rate per man and maybe a rough estimate of the time required for the job, with no commitment whatsoever.

In highly standardised environments such as the construction industry, an estimator can make reasonable assumptions about how the building has been built. By referring to standards, he can guess the thickness of a wall, the spacing of the studs or the presence of concrete blocks behind the wall. Moreover, at least for commercial and institutional buildings, the estimator will probably have access to the original blueprints and other design documents to help understand what lies behind the visible parts.

If the builder discovers after the work begins that the construction does not comply with the original blueprints or that the construction standards were not followed, he will stop immediately, call the architect and the customer, explain the issue and demand a formal change order, since it is always assumed that the building is compliant with blueprints and construction codes.

But in your organization's IT function, things are quite different in several ways. To begin with, standards are nonexistent, incomplete or not enforced. Next, the documentation is likely incomplete. The fact is, your IT team is not scrupulously documenting what is being delivered, which adversely affects future generations of IT staff who are trying to understand your assets.

This laxity does not originate from some sort of repugnance toward documentation, but from the fundamental project-orientation of your IT organization. First, documents that describe how your IT assets are built and work are always created through projects. Second, documents that favor project delivery are more important than other documents. That's because documents created via projects can be divided into two broad categories:

a)   those that help in the process of building the solution; and

b)   those that describe the end result that was built.

The former category is required for facilitating communication between teams and stakeholders, ensuring plans are put on paper first, then validated, approved and understood before the actual building work starts. The rationale here is that changing one's mind about requirements or design once the building phase has begun costs much more than when they're just ink on paper.

The latter category has a very different objective: allowing the operators, users, maintainers and future teams of designers and builders to understand what was actually put in place.

In the case of the first category, the documents' quality and completeness is directly related to the efficiency of the project. If too much time is spent documenting, the budget and schedule may be directly and negatively impacted. However, if the documentation is not done well, or is too superficial and lacks the necessary details, the project's budget and schedule will also be adversely impacted by such things as misunderstandings between teams, delayed approvals, or the worst of evils, rework.

Project delivery documents are taken care of by project teams in a reasonable fashion for one reason: because they impact project delivery which is a measured performance criteria in project-oriented IT.

The documents of the second category represent a legacy for forthcoming projects and future generations of IT staff. They will be used to understand how the solution works on the inside (since not much can be assumed from standards that do not exist or aren't enforced).

On the one hand, these "end result" documents will speed up estimation as well as the time spent modifying the solution in subsequent projects. But on the other hand, such documentation adds no direct customer value to the current project deliverables.

If anything can be cut without impacting the workability and business effectiveness of the solution, documentation is an easy target. It is the first task to hit the back burner when delivery pressures mount or IT personnel are moved to a more pressing project.

With incomplete records of end solutions being the norm, the question begs to be asked: Who benefits from poorly documented IT assets? Not you the paying customer, that's for sure. Poor documentation leads to greater time and energy spent by future IT staff desperately trying to understand the current asset they're dealing with. And time is money.

Of course, the internal quality control (QC) team might have documentation on their checklist, but they usually lack the independence and incentives required to ensure anything other than the project's success. What's more, the QC team simply doesn't possess the required skills to assess the completeness of many documents.

Unfortunately, anything that has to do with future projects — like end result documentation — is often relegated to *best effort*, or in other words, to whomever has the spare time to complete it.

If you believe that the use of external or internal standards is the solution to this issue, you're absolutely right. However, IT is stuck in an operating mode where defining quality standards and abiding by them is severely deficient.

No Rescue From Standards

Uniformity Is the Key to Achieving Minimal Quality Levels and Reducing Inefficiencies. Unfortunately, the Engagement Model Impedes a Successful Definition of Standards.

There are two fundamental intents behind IT standards:

1. Sustain the quality of IT work above certain minimal levels; and

2. Reduce the variety of technologies, processes or techniques to be knowledgeable about.

Regarding the first point, minimal quality levels cannot be attained if they are not initially defined. You cannot simply ask your IT staff to do good work and keep getting better without defining what "good work" entails for your organization. That's where standards come to the rescue.

The second point has to do with variety. With the IT industry in general being quite dynamic, there are formidable forces pulling your IT function towards heterogeneity[27]. In addition to compulsive buyers (Chapter 4) and siloed teams (Chapters 2), there are armies of advertisers, peddlers and other direct marketers that are bombarding IT folks with messages about their panaceas and miracle solutions. I personally receive emails and unsolicited cold calls on an almost weekly basis, even when I am not in a decision-making position for purchasing.

But the more variety there is, the more trouble IT is in. The more heterogeneity in IT assets, the more costly projects and

---

[27] *That's the fancy word for an unmanageable buffet of disjointed information technologies.*

maintenance will be. There is no way to escape this causality. IT staff has to be hired, trained, retained and backed-up during vacation, and the more technologies they use, the more costly it becomes. Resources will be less exchangeable with heterogeneity. Incompatible technologies need to interact with one another, adding more work to palliate the conflicts. Overall, having more technologies, methods or approaches just adds more work in order to get things done (Figure 15).

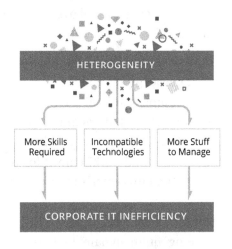

Figure 15 - Heterogeneity, Source of Inefficiencies

Let me be very clear: heterogeneity's wickedness is not rooted in an idealistic view of your IT systems. It is nothing less than a calamity that is costing you a good share of your annual IT spending. Heterogeneity, if not vigorously contained, is making your IT team inefficient and slowing its delivery of value-add change.

So how can it be energetically harnessed? There is only one way: standardizing. And through standardization, quality levels will in turn be taken care of.

Unfortunately, the solution is not as easy as it sounds, because standards in the dynamic world of IT are rarely usable as-is.

The Indispensable Customization

Quality standards need to cover a large spectrum of topics that can be divided into the following three areas of focus: what your IT purchases, how your IT team works[28], and how solutions are built.

For the purchasing part, your IT team is probably already in good shape. When it comes to buying from third parties, the roles are well defined: you buy, they build and support. And since it has been that way for decades for commercially available software and hardware, things are much easier. Benchmarks, checklists, vendor reviews, cross-industry standards, or magic quadrants[29] can safeguard you. Most of your IT infrastructure falls under this first category.

For the second and third categories (the way IT folks work and the way they build solutions) it's another story.

Because there are holes in the coverage of existing standards, some areas have little matter to begin with. Standards sometimes come too late for leading-edge IT projects that deal with new concepts and technologies. The breadth of standards your IT team can rely on does not cover the span of work they have to do. In many areas, especially the more recent or leading-edge technologies, standards are nonexistent. It is a *terra incognita* in which they have to go because of market pressures. Or perhaps it's where they want to go because it is the newest and hottest technology that sells on a CV[30].

---

[28] *Such as ITIL[48] for operations, CMMI[46] for application development, or one of the many project management methods available from consulting firms, or internally grown by your organization.*

[29] *Referring to the famous Magic Quadrants from Gartner.*

[30] *My experience in the trenches is that you should not underestimate the extent of heterogeneity or debatable decisions created by this driver.*

Some of the standards are too shallow to be used effectively in real day-to-day IT and, while serving as a base, need to be further detailed. Most of the standards I have dealt with were good starters, delineating an area of IT knowledge and providing guidelines, but they usually did not suffice. They had to be further detailed, down to a level where the average IT worker could use the technology in such a way that heterogeneity could really be contained and that acceptable levels of quality in the work could be achieved.

An important point about some standards is that they should be viewed as the lowest common denominator for an industry. Some standards are proven recipes for old problems. If you simply want these problems to be solved or want to avoid falling into known traps, then these standards are fine. But your organization could get a competitive edge by developing a better, more powerful standard. Something that is applied systematically, like any standard, but not shared with competitors. This is a viable option if your IT department drives towards gathering, adapting or building its own set of standards.

The key to developing a successful set of customized standards for your organization is centralization.

One and Only One

Standards-setting in your IT organization must be centralized. Leaving it to several teams will generate unwanted behaviors.

First, standards must be unique and applied by all IT staff to achieve the benefits your company is looking for. Multiple, competing standards just won't work.

Secondly, if standards-setting is left to several teams, the choice will be influenced by the skills and knowledge of the IT people in each group. Having all IT teams using the same tools and following the same processes is the ultimate goal. If one team using a different technology composes 10% of the IT staff and the other 90% are using another standard for the same purpose, then demanding the smaller team to switch makes a lot of sense. Whatever the case, standardization means that some teams will have to join the ranks of the majority, whether they like it or not. Thirdly, if left to several teams, chances are that standards-setting will not be their main performance objective. If the teams are primarily measured on things other than standards-setting, coverage or compliance, you can be sure that a missing guideline will rarely be considered as an urgent obligation for correcting the situation.

If the responsibility of defining IT standards is spread across many IT teams, it will be frequently outdated and most probably incomplete. This prevalent lack of motivation among IT teams to set standards deserves a deeper look.

Who Wants Them Anyhow?

Your IT department does not build servers or computers: they buy them from external, third-party vendors.

Not surprisingly, corporate IT teams have become tough customers that have forced the whole computing infrastructure industry to standardize. The positive result today is that the infrastructure portion of your corporate IT is undoubtedly the most mature of all in terms of the existence of standards and the effective compliance to them.

If vendors were not forced by customers and market pressures to comply with standards, they simply wouldn't do it. Being the only vendor on the planet who can fulfill a customer's needs because other vendors aren't offering compatible products is a great way to trap your customer for a long time. Does this sound familiar?

Why create standardized products that a customer can replace with a competitor's equivalent? Why create products that can be benchmarked and easily compared with the rivals? No, compliance to standards does not come naturally to the party that makes a living at building custom solutions. How good can an IT team be at defining and enforcing standards for solutions they create and provide to the rest of your business?

If responsible for all of this, that team will be doing poorly with standards compliance, since it has no direct impact on their most important performance indicators. Worse, building highly-customized systems with nonstandard technologies and methods that only one team in the world can understand and support is the perfect way to lock-in a customer for a long period of time.

Don't get me wrong, there is no gigantic plot at work here. These are just ordinary IT people that have a mortgage to pay, managed by individuals who understand that the IT corporate ladder is climbed by having more employees[31].

In my career, I have seen dozens of cases where a team develops a solution almost identical to that of another team without even knowing it. Most of the time, the two teams worked on the same floor. No, defining standards and abiding by them

---

[31] *In IT, just like any other field, the size of the managed team is one of the most monetarily rewarded indicators of personal performance for managers.*

does not come naturally, or there is a good reason, whether it's market dynamics or coercion. Unless you can simulate market pressures in your own internal IT department, the only path to standardization is obligation.

Are your IT standards, as in so many organizations, posted on the intranet, in hopes that hundreds of IT staff will have the time and interest to read them? Probably so. Is there time and effort spent to educate IT teams about the standards? Probably not enough.

Standards-setting and quality control are intimately linked. The first step to mitigating this is to put in place tighter quality controls that force the adoption of standards and compliance in IT work products. But as we shall see next, controlling quality is not easy when accountabilities are improperly assigned.

Uncontrolled Quality

Compliance to Quality Standards Works Only When It Positively Affects Measured Performance Objectives.

Quality Control (QC) on IT projects has been common practice for as long as information technologies have been around. It is one of the best ways to ensure that solutions are up to quality standards and stimulate improvement.

The quality standards may vary, depending on the importance of the end product. For example, the effort, science and time spent on QC for an airborne aircraft monitoring system will be much more extensive than the QC on an information-only website.

Quality control includes all types of checks, performed not only on the end product but also during the design and building processes, to verify that expected results or standards are met. Quality control can be done on the portion that you see, as well as on many less-visible aspects, such as databases, impact on other applications, performance under loads, security and intrusion, simulated crash tests and more.

An endless number of elements can be checked for quality, hence it is mandatory to make a plan of what will be checked, to what extent, against which quality standards and at what frequency in order to keep a grip on the costs associated with quality control. That plan is called the *quality management plan* of a project.

Because quality control costs money, sound budget management is crucial and encourages the development of quality management plans that tackle high-impact quality issues first.

So what is important enough for your IT teams to put in place the processes and tools to detect quality issues? As depicted in Table 2, at the highest level there are two kinds of drivers for quality control: (A) what is related to your expectations (you the sponsor); and (B) what impacts IT's true accountabilities (the measured ones). In other words, satisfy customer expectations regarding the delivered product and meet measured performance levels.

Table 2 - Drivers-of-Quality Criteria

A Meet the requirements	1 - Stable solution
	2 - Performant solution
	3 - Does what it is expected to do
B Align with accountabilities	1 - Operational stability
	2 - System's performance
	3 - On-time and on-budget delivery

The first category of drivers can be summarized by these two questions: Does it work properly? Does it support the business processes as expected?

The Quality That Matters

The most important IT performance indicators are those related to systems availability, stability and performance[32]. Therefore, quality controls that will reduce the probability of software crashes, performance degradation or unavailability of applications will be taken very seriously and are at the top of the list of important controls.

When such defects are identified, they probably get a Severity 1[28] grade. If, for any reason, the project schedule is tightened or funding is cut, these tests will be the last ones that IT would want to cut corners on. I can guess that your IT team might simply refuse to deliver the solution if those tests are not performed, even under executive threats.

---

[32] As we saw in Chapter 3.

For any quality issue of the Severity 1 type, let me reassure you that all IT organizations take this seriously and put in place the quality control processes, automations and skills to minimize such occurrences.

Project teams will perform all sorts of tests on the resulting applications: programmers will test their code, then independent testers will execute other tests, then users will complete their own tests, and finally machines will simulate a population of users to measure performance and stability.

All of this will be done first in laboratory environments, and then in special "guarded" environments that are copies of the real thing for business users. In other words, plenty of science will be put into carrying out effective testing to ensure there are no crashes, no outages and no slow response times.

These quality checks cover drivers A-1, A-2, B-1 and B-2 in Table 2 above. These controls help to both meet your expectations with respect to the solution and support IT's most important and well-measured accountabilities.

The next most important (and measured) accountability after operational performance and stability is project performance, which boils down to budget and calendar. On-time and on-budget are the core indicators that reveal the true achievers. Moreover, and contrary to some other project delivery metrics, time and money are easy to count and well-understood concepts.

I can guarantee that your IT team puts a lot of effort into establishing the necessary tasks, documents, processes, skills, tools and governance mechanisms to ensure that budget is managed tightly and delivery dates are tracked. They will hire seasoned project managers, demand industry certifications such as PMP[33] or CSM[34], implement project risk management, perform thorough time management, and track and validate every hour charged and every penny spent.

That's why quality controls will diligently be applied to anything that may jeopardize project performance with delays or additional costs. These controls cover drivers B-3 of course, but also driver A-3 in Table 2, because if the solution does not meet business requirements, the inevitable result will be delays and additional costs to fix it, since there is no point in delivering an IT solution if it does not do what it is supposed to do.

Many things can cause delays or increased project costs. A misunderstood business rule or the meaning of a data item may lead to rework during the project. For an IT project manager, rework means working twice on something that was planned to be done only once. There is usually a contingency budget and time set aside for unpredictable situations, but never enough to do things twice, especially with all the other things that can go wrong, such as resource unavailability or plain oversights.

And indeed, in complex IT environments, one may very well miss small or bigger issues that arise during the project. For example, a third business partner interface that no one had thought of, a fifth customer information file that was not documented, an old and hardly used system that is not yet retired but is still required for regulatory reporting. Oversights are always hiding where you can't see them.

---

[33] *Project Management Professionals[44]*
[34] *Certified Scrum Masters[45]*

Since nobody's perfect and oversights are quite frequent, the project teams scrupulously document all that needs to be done and make it the official and assumed scope. Project teams will ensure the documents that specify what has to be done are crystal clear. Not only will this help identify missing elements or errors, but it will also help make assumptions on the scope of the project. Anything outside of it will therefore be deemed out-of-scope and will be subject to change orders. Hence, when a fifth customer information file is "discovered," the scope of the project will need to be modified, a change order issued, and the project budget and schedule revised accordingly. Remember, when change orders are accepted, the on-time-on-budget performance indicators are not affected since they always calculated on the attainment of figures made from the initial estimates (the *baseline*[29]), plus all variations coming from change orders.

Projects will go to substantial lengths with formal processes, rigorous documentation, and stringent quality controls to ensure oversights that could blow-up the budget and schedule are identified.

The Quality Control of the Rest

Now, what about the design decisions that affect neither IT operations nor cost and schedule of the projects, but lead to convoluted and hard to maintain solutions? For example, sub-optimal architectures and designs that lead to a lack of agility and speed in the delivery of business solutions. Shouldn't your IT simply have more stringent project quality controls so that this doesn't happen?

Not really.

The sad but true answer is that when identified and if they are communicated, they will be recognized as issues, but not managed like other quality issues.[35] Any quality issue that does not strictly fit the criteria in Table 2 is considered second class and will be tossed at the first sign of jeopardizing the OTOB objective.

In all organizations I've worked with, there was an internal committee usually labelled as the Architecture Review Board (ARB[36]). It was composed mainly of IT architects and other senior IT stakeholders that reviewed all architectures for their compliance to policies, principles and standards of all sorts that touch a series of subjects, from preferred vendors, products, programing languages, tools, methods and practices. However, in my view, the effectiveness of the ARB ranged from positively accepted consultancy down to tolerated annoyance.

All architecture compliance review processes come with a dispensation process to account for exceptional conditions. But when budget constraints become an exceptional condition, project managers and other senior IT managers involved in the design and construction of the solution know the rules of the game: architecture reviews are a necessary evil, but can always be bypassed.

In the construction industry, if a city inspector finds that a given standard hasn't been followed, he has the power, if the gravity warrants it, to stop everything immediately and demand that the builder dismantle forthwith the faulty component and redo it. The inspector is entirely independent and has absolutely no interest in the builder's construction schedule issues or tight profit margins.

---

[35] It falls in The Rest category depicted in Figure 11 in Chapter 3.
[36] The ARB label is pretty standard throughout the industry. You probably have one active in your IT organization.

No matter how well-defined your standards are, if the people in charge of ensuring solution compliance are put into the untenable position of biting the hand that feeds them, you are bound to have a number of nonstandard solutions coming out of a loose net. And these types of solutions are those that make your corporate IT a complexity factory. Do not count on your review board to save you from ill-designed solutions that perpetuate convolution.

The Quality Dead End

And there is more bad news. You have a system in place that puts your IT team in a lose-lose situation. Here is how it works.

If a quality control process does not help reduce the risks of not meeting requirements or jeopardizing measured accountabilities (drivers A & B in Table 2 above) then it defaults to a project cost like any other. Quality controls need effort, and as such they have a price tag like the rest. Since project budget and schedule are bound to be tight, the quality control effort and cost is in direct competition with other project activities. When the time comes to make hard choices to reduce budget or schedule, these activities won't stand a chance against all the others for which there is an immediate, palatable benefit for the project.

The reciprocal conclusion is that any quality control, or to a larger extent any IT best practice, that has a beneficial impact outside of project delivery will be considered at best as a desirable virtue, but will inevitably be eliminated from the project's scope at the first sign of a risk to the project.

Questionable decisions that negatively affect the resulting IT asset's flexibility and adaptability to business changes are almost systematically materialized through projects. But they rarely have a negative impact on the project itself or any other of the top accountabilities of your IT team.

The result is that no one is really addressing these issues (by tackling, changing and solving them) because there are no incentives to do so, and worse, there are incentives to not address them.

As long as on-time and on-budget remain the top performance measures with attached incentives, your internal IT factory will continue to diligently produce, year after year, million-dollar solutions in which agility, sustainability or asset value were never really considered.

This is not due to some laxity or lack of knowledge on the part of corporate IT staff about quality criteria that have a long-term, cross-project, positive impact on IT assets. It's all about how accountabilities are distributed. Those who are in charge of controlling quality are sleeping in the same bed as those who build what has to be controlled. In addition, the IT performance measures are colliding with a whole section of the quality criteria that extends far beyond project boundaries and into asset management.

When assets aren't treated as such, quality standards and control are bound to also be treated lightly. In the next section, you will discover that managing IT's work products as assets is also challenged by conflicting roles, which leads to a lower-quality end result.

Assets? What Assets?

Corporate IT's Incentives Are Focused On Operational and Project Expenses, Not Asset Investment

Remember your boutique hotel plumbing issues in Chapter 4? One of the main issues was the sink's nonstandard pipes that needed to be replaced. Merely measuring the time and cost of replacing sinks is not enough to justify standardizing pipe diameters, pipe material and pipe pressure. One has to be able to measure the time spent manufacturing custom fittings or the price of purchasing and installing the regulator, plus the additional time spent by the plumber to diagnose the problem, get the parts, and travel back and forth. If costs are collected and then reported as the average time to install a sink, how can you raise awareness about the importance of putting in place regulations and standards that are focused on pipes?

Conversely, how can you convince a business sponsor to invest in sustainable IT asset development if you cannot show figures about time lost in low-value tasks? You need a way to identify the cost of activities that provide absolutely no business value, lengthen projects and augment costs as a result of ill-designed components or overly complex assets.

Custom-made pipe fittings cost money and add absolutely no value. Your hotel guests need good-looking and functional sinks. They could not care less about hidden regulators and tailor-made pipe fittings. The former brings real value, while the latter just brings additional costs and delays.

Project cost data is primarily collected through timesheets, and timesheet structures usually match the project schedule. This is important because the project manager needs to link staff effort with a schedule that shows the attainment of major milestones[37]. Hence, the description in timesheets of the work performed will match the project's schedule labels, such as "Phase 1," "Phase 2" or "Sprint 5." This is fine for managing projects, but is not great help for identifying how much time is spent on low-value activities.

If I want to convince the Guild of Boutique Hotel Owners (GOBOH) in my allegory that they need to demand that new hotels be designed and built according to a single standard as well as hire special inspectors who will make sure that all new plumbing is compliant, I'd better have hard numbers detailing the savings on custom-fitting manufacturing and pressure-regulator costs.

In the last three decades I have not only filled thousands of time-sheets, but also created timesheets for team members in specific projects, as well as templates for project offices. In one engagement, I went through hundreds of thousands of weekly timesheets, filtering, grouping and cross-referencing data. Believe me, it was a smorgasbord of everything under the sun because timesheets were left to dozens of project managers with no standard to frame the choices. It was simply unusable to draw any convincing, quantified story about the costs of the no-added-value activities or the too-costly components that should be retired.

Let me be clear on one thing: sound project management should always be supported by cost data collection processes that are aligned with the projects themselves. Whatever you do in that area should remain as good as it is. But there is more than project management to measure.

---

[37] *There are several project management metrics to help assess the progress of a project or estimate what's left to do, and if the schedule will be respected or not, such as the earned value concept[43], but they are all based on the existence of project plans and rarely on the assets used, modified or created.*

Think for a moment about the business you're in, whether it be transportation, telecoms, banking, etc. Now think about all the processes you develop, the systems you put in place and all the intelligence you deploy to track costs. Think about the huge data warehouses you have invested in to track pounds or tons of this, square foot of that, railroad miles, claims, mortgages, phone calls, accounts, clients, dollars here, pennies there. Your business survival depends largely upon understanding where the money goes.

How does it compare to what your corporate IT team does in terms of tracking its own costs when creating and enhancing IT assets? I bet your IT tracking looks like this: spreadsheets detailing hundreds of thousands of man-hours in project columns, high-level sketchy mappings ascribing those millions of dollars to pseudo-assets called systems, named applications or portfolios, none of which match the real assets that are effectively built at the technical level.

To help you understand, take a look at Figure 16.

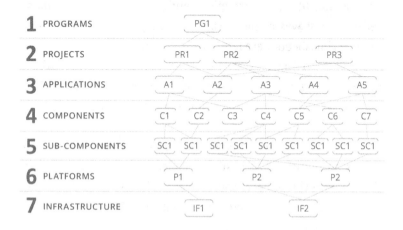

Figure 16 - What You See and What's Below It

Now please, don't run away! It may look like complex IT geek stuff, but believe me, it's simple to understand. It reads from left to right and top to bottom. I have numbered each layer from 1 at the top to 7 at the bottom. The only thing that I'd like you to understand is that layers 1 to 3 (programs, projects and applications) are the ones you, as a non-IT decision maker, will be exposed to. And that's fine because layers 4 to 7 are technical by nature.

But there's something really important about these layers: on a day-to-day basis, your IT staff is not creating any of layers 1 to 3. Yes, you read it right. What they're really working on are layers 4 and below. From a technical point of view, the layers above number 4 are needed simply to facilitate communications. On any given work day, IT staff do not sit in front of their computers and work on your CRM or your billing system or your websites. The actual IT work is much more compartmented than applications or projects. It also means that your IT assets are not applications: they are a collection of interacting technical components. Please stay with me, we're almost finished; I promise!

On the right-hand side, the lines and boxes show that applications are a collection of components, which are made of a collection of sub-components. Those sub-components use other finer-grained components that in turn require platforms that require infrastructure to operate. The important point to remember here is that the further you go into the layers, the more they are shared by the layers above. The more you dive into the details, the more you see that it's a web of inter-related and shared assets. That's a wanted virtue: sharing and reusing is a sign of flexible and well-designed IT assets. The more your assets are shared or reused, the lesser the chances that you have paid multiple time to get the same thing[38].

---

[38] As you saw in Chapter 4 on the Complexity Factory.

In the end, you simply cannot relate each asset to applications, let alone projects. Because lower-level components are shared by the layers above, rolling-up costs to applications doesn't work: you'd count multiple times the costs of the lower levels in the higher ones.

Corporate IT's reason to exist is not to deliver projects. Their mission is to put in place solutions, systems, components and sub-components. In short, IT's purpose is to spawn IT assets that support your business —projects are simply a means to get there.

At the end of the year, your IT function would have a hard time showing you the list of assets created or enhanced and how much money was "invested" in them. The best they can do is approximate expenditures on a high-level list of applications. And even when they do, the figures will be wrong, because the numbers originate from processes and tools that collect and ventilate costs for the main purpose of managing projects, not the components that represent the real assets.

Neither can your IT team evaluate the total lifetime value of the IT assets you have invested in. They can add up project, program and portfolio costs from a few years back, but you must then make the leap to matching said costs to assets. Your corporate IT is not in the asset business.

Hence, your IT function doesn't really know where the money goes in the assets that they create and maintain. And if they can't tell where the asset money goes, they just don't know their assets, period.

Your project money is supposed to create something, not just be expenditure in next year's statement of income. But year after year, corporate IT is delivering projects, while remaining quite ignorant about the real cost of what they've constructed.

For six years I have worked for an IT department supporting an airline. There was a very knowledgeable and effective IT team supporting aircraft maintenance processes with a set of applications that tracked almost everything done on an airplane.

If an airline company can track the number of flight hours and detailed maintenance activities on thousands of aircraft parts and on hundreds of airplanes, then why doesn't your IT shop track hours spent on a few hundred components?

The answer is simple: there are no incentives to do so.

Will it help stabilize systems and reduce outages and down times? Not really. Could it help reduce wait time on the IT help line? No. Will it help project delivery? No again.

In the airline transportation industry, there are external and independent bodies overseeing aircraft maintenance. If a company cannot show proof of compliance with respect to parts maintenance, inspection or replacement, aircrafts can be grounded, no discussion. That's a pretty effective incentive.

The objective of project-oriented IT[39] is to deliver according to the planned budget and schedule, not to manage total cost of ownership of assets.

---

[39] As we saw in Chapter 5.

What happens after the delivery of the last phase of a project is of lesser importance to IT.

External bodies overseeing your IT assets are not coming anytime soon. In the meantime, the lever you're left with is to ensure assets are not managed by the same teams that are accountable for delivering projects on-time and on-budget.

Collecting costs data about assets has quite a different objective: gaining valuable insight into what is created. That is, valuable management information on the tangible things that are created, worked on, maintained or retired.

In order for processes to be put in place to define what assets are and collect relevant data about how much they cost over projects and over years, someone has to be accountable for it. But beware, it will never work if you assign yet another accountability to individuals who also have promotions and bonuses attached to delivering projects on-time and on-budget.

True asset management is not just about having accurate metrics detailing where the money goes, knowing if standards are defined, and controlling quality levels. Asset management is also about intelligence and keeping a firm grip on the IT investments in place.

Deep and quantified knowledge about your IT assets has a direct impact on project success, as you will see next.

CHAPTER SIX TAKEAWAYS

- *Because your IT is project-oriented, entire sections of the documentation of your investments are left to good intentions.*

- *Standardizing what is purchased and how things are done in IT is imperative to reduce heterogeneity, a patent cause of inefficiencies.*

- *Identifying, choosing and adapting standards has to be centralized and assigned to someone without conflicting accountabilities.*

- *Quality controls need to expand to all the standards your assets should reach, beyond the sole support of project performance.*

- *Your IT function needs to evolve from managing budgeted expenses to managing all its assets.*

7. ESTIMATION DEFICIT DISORDER

Unmanaged IT Assets Create Uncertainty That Impacts Project Success. The Engagement Model Further Cripples the Estimation Practice.

Managing IT assets, their lifecycles and their quality levels isn't about declaring that processes are in place for managing IT investment in a sustainable way. The objective is to give corporate IT data, information, knowledge and insights about their creations and leverage them to reduce risk. Reducing unknowns can lead to better estimation of impacts, of investment magnitude and of time to deliver.

How projects are appraised is directly impacted by the estimator's knowledge about the assets in place. Shallow asset cost-gathering processes lead to a limited understanding of asset composition. If assets are loosely mapped to applications, but applications aren't the real IT assets, they're not much help. If asset costs are not tracked because all the cost gathering information is project-oriented, it becomes difficult to understand and evaluate the complexity of the work to be done.

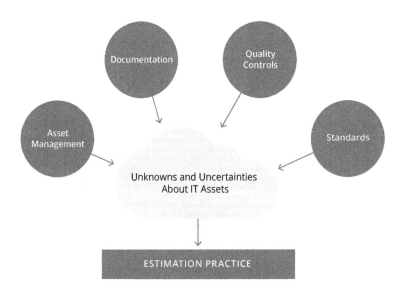

Figure 17 - Asset Unknowns That Subvert Estimation

Additionally, entire portions of quality control are left to good intentions, resulting in unreliable assumptions about how the asset is built. There is always a chance that a small, nonstandard element could blow-up estimates done in good faith. With quality controls on documentation also being challenged, estimators cannot rely on documented specifications either.

Poor standards definition, poor quality controls, poor documentation and poor asset knowledge create a lot of unknowns for people that need to estimate the work to be done (Figure 17).

As if this wasn't enough, the efficiency of IT estimation is challenged from many other angles as well.

Estimation is not an easy task and requires hard work, discipline, method and experience. As an IT insider, estimation is one of my favorite areas of sub-optimal behaviors because of the high impact it has on project success — your success — and the very little visibility this practice gets outside of IT.

Given the poor track record of IT projects[40], one would be naturally tempted to say that IT departments should just get better at estimating to improve their track record. Unfortunately, it's not that simple.

To better understand estimation, let's take a quick look at the array of techniques made available to IT in the last decades for estimating time and schedule[41]:

1. *Algorithmic modeling,* which provides one or more algorithms and their cost-driving parameters.

2. *Expert judgment,* which involves consulting one or more experts to get cost estimates.

3. *Analogy,* which involves reasoning with analogies from completed projects to derive an estimate for the new project.

4. *Parkinson's law,* which applies a principle where cost estimate equate to the available resources (available money, time or skills).

5. *Price to win,* where the cost estimate equates to what is believed necessary to win the job (or have the project ready for a specific date).

6. *Top-down,* where a global cost is estimated (with another technique) and then split into the various components.

7. *Bottom-up,* where each component is evaluated separately (with another technique) and the costs aggregated.

---

[40] *Assuming that your mind is made-up on the subject. If not, I've added a few notes [48] at the end.*

[41] *Taken from the most respected reference on the subject[35].*

These techniques come with the following basic, down-to-earth recommendations:

- Do not use techniques #4 and #5.

- Always use a combination of at least two techniques.

- Collect data about costs and cost drivers, both estimated and actual.

But in most IT organizations that are project-oriented, the systematic collection of cost data is not about what was estimated, but what it effectively ended up costing, on a project-by-project basis. I have never seen, read, nor heard of systematic data collection about the estimation process itself and the assumptions and cost drivers that were used.

How is your IT organization managing the estimation process and practices? Is it building an estimation algorithm that is revisited and fine-tuned every year based on actuals? Is it using several of the types of estimation techniques above? Is it implementing continuous improvement in estimation through six sigma techniques?

Perhaps your IT organization uses a variation of the "Price to Win" technique by always providing estimates that fit within the business schedule or available budget.

My personal experience has shown that the project estimation:

- is frequently left to project managers or IT managers;

- may be based on standard *proportions* for phases of a project;

- is based on one estimation technique only;

- is not based on an algorithmic technique; and

- is not subject to the systematic collection and use of historical data.

I was stunned by the discussions I had with a representative from a commercial real estate independent valuation practice. These firms do nothing else but estimating and tracking costs and return on investment for construction projects. They track every possible cost item, from land to permits to concrete to steel, nails and lumber. And then they cross-reference it to all that is imaginable for that industry: customer, building types, standards compliance, locations, etc. They pride themselves on the huge amount of data they collect for decades of construction projects, as well as the state-of-the-art estimation software they develop. Given all the skills available in the IT field to collect and analyze data, I felt embarrassed by the ludicrous Stone Age tools that corporate IT uses.

For corporate IT organizations that deliver business solutions, estimation processes are quite unsophisticated. Surely, other fields benefit from more standards and do not have the "privilege" of being able to make anything work in a virtual world, but it is worth asking why the IT project estimation practice in your organization, as I confidently suspect, is still in its infancy and seems to be permanently stalled.

If someone in your IT organization ever tries to convince you of the difficulties of building a reliable estimation process due to the newness and lack of maturity in IT, here's an interesting quote to consider from:

*"False scheduling to match the patron's desired date is
much more common in our discipline than elsewhere
in engineering. It is difficult to make a vigorous, plau-
sible, and job-risking defense of an estimate that is
derived by no quantitative method, supported by little
data, and certified chiefly by hunches of the managers.
[...] Until estimating is on a sounder basis, individual
managers will need to stiffen their backbones, and
defend their estimates with the assurance that their
poor hunches are better than wish-derived estimates."*

Readers who have an intimate knowledge of the forces that
drive the estimation process of IT projects may think this is an
excerpt from a blog or a recent report from one of the IT obser-
vatories. These statements are quite apropos and contemporary
in the world of IT.

But here's the embarrassment: this quote is from a landmark
book, *The Mythical Man-Month*[20], published in 1975!

Since the days when I was playing street hockey in front of my
parents' house with other 10-year-old boys, software estimation techniques have evolved. Today, IT professionals can find a
wealth of publications, training courses and tools to help them
implement costing models specialized for software development and application integration[30][31].

Then why is it that IT groups within organizations that have spent
hundreds of millions of dollars over the past decade in business

solutions development and integration are so poorly equipped to evaluate IT project costs despite their notorious underachievement in managing projects that are on-time and on-budget?

How can such a serious weakness, with such considerable monetary consequences, not be the driver of a relentless quest for improvement? The answer is simple: there are no incentives to do so.

First and foremost, there is no competition. There might be cases where alternatives like developing internally with existing assets and teams or purchasing a packaged application are being looked at, but it is fair to say that in general, lines of business sponsors are in competition for a limited annual amount of investment money, but the IT side doesn't compete.

Secondly, in other fields estimation errors have one very significant impact on the estimating party: losing money. If bidders inflate their cost estimation and add exaggerated buffers, they will most likely not win the contract. And if they really want the contract and end up underbidding, they will truly lose money.

One may also try to convince you that there is one major difference between the IT business solution's delivery practice and other engineering fields: much more time is spent in architecture and design phases in IT projects.

The impact on the estimation process is huge: it takes more time and more money to come to a point where the design of what needs to be built is final. The identification of the final requirements to be implemented is pushed further in time, adding another complication to the estimation process.

Recognizing the specific challenges that IT faces with its estimating practice is one thing, but using it as an excuse to perpetuate poor estimation techniques is another.

Regardless of the existence of such challenges particular to IT, the fact remains that the money comes from a customer who needs to know how much the project is going to cost, because without knowledge of the investment magnitude, the project simply won't be funded in the first place.

In the end, the consequences of wrong estimates are relatively benign for corporate IT teams. There is no direct loss of money on the part of the estimating party. The worst that could happen is the project gets cancelled, possibly impacting IT resources if there are no other projects to keep them busy. There is no contractual agreement to force the IT team to complete the job for the agreed-upon price.

Unless it is in a call-for-bids mode, the business sponsor has very little means of assessing the precision or rigor behind the estimates. In a bidding mode, the estimates from different builders can be compared, but not when the business sponsor is bound to its own internal IT. When competition is in action, those who create the specifications are not the same as those who provide the estimates and should not have any relationship or interest with the bidders, or else competition wouldn't be in action.

The IT engagement model does not have the same healthy balance that is found in the construction industry, for example. The team that defines the specifications and the team that builds the solution most likely have the same boss at some point in the hierarchy.

This often leads to unwanted behaviors, such as overly optimistic estimates and permissiveness in noncompliance to specifications, as well as skewed designs that favor the building team's strengths and limitations, but detrimental to the value of the resulting asset.

There is no centralized IT estimation practice per se; this activity is left to the various teams. No custom quantitative estimation models are developed and maintained, and no data is collected with the clear objective of improving estimation over the years.

Because the IT organization is primarily accountable for being on-time and on-budget, and never for the precision of its estimates, and because there are no serious consequences to poor estimation, little effort is put into standardization, data collection, predictive model development and all other good practices that could help improve estimates.

The absence of real incentives leads to a poor estimation practice, which leads to poor project estimates, cutting corners to abide by those estimates and to lower-quality solutions and assets.

And here we are, closing the vicious circle: lower-quality assets that in turn fuel poor estimation that consecutively incites the creation of low-quality assets. Improving the cost evaluation function could break that spiral. The issue of IT's poor estimation practice is not a result of IT folks not knowing how to improve a process — that's dead center in IT's core competencies.

No, the issue lies in IT people having more urgent tasks to complete instead of improving themselves in that area.

CHAPTER SEVEN TAKEAWAYS

- *By improving asset management, documentation, standards definition and quality control we can reduce unknowns and improve the project estimation practice.*

- *The only way for corporate IT to raise its estimation practice maturity to the level you deserve is to change how accountabilities and the accompanying measures are distributed.*

CONCLUSION

In the preceding chapters, we have gone through the sequence of causes and effects that afflict corporate IT and, in the end, impede business agility and speed. They are summarized in Figure 18.

The speed at which the business can change is bogged down by the ever-growing complexity of IT systems already in place. These are the so-called assets created in past projects that come back to haunt your IT function. No matter how hard your IT staff work at it, they will always have an inadequate knowledge about the systems in place, thus hindering their speed to deliver. Poor documentation, weak standardization and incomplete quality controls not only fuel complexity, they augment the risks on the timely delivery of your digital solutions. Any change is hampered.

But it doesn't have to be that way. Quality can be attained. Complexity can be contained.

Complexity is fed by the various types of silos that fill the corporate IT horizon: budgetary silos, team silos and the most harmful, project-orientation. Silos have existed forever, and putting in place cross-cutting mechanisms is not rocket science.

Complexity is also fed by faint asset management. Except for what is bought from third parties, your corporate IT manages expenses, not assets. And that's regardless of where you put them in your financial ledgers. The absence of appropriate asset management practices has a direct impact on the quality of what is resulting from your investments in technology, especially in the case of unnecessary complexity. When you know that what is put in place will be there for a long period of time, the criteria for quality expands far beyond immediate delivery obligations.

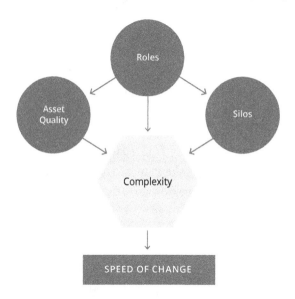

Figure 18 - The Path to Killing Business-Change Speed

Incomplete quality controls, weak asset management, unharnessed silo cultures and pullulating complexity all take their source in conflicting roles and what surrounds them: delineation of responsibilities, accountabilities upon results, measures of attainment of outcomes and the processes that support it all.

Corporate IT people solve your problems with the help of information technology. That's their mission and that's within their comfort zone. The issues put forth in this first volume have lingered for decades, not because corporate IT staff aren't capable of solving the various problems, but because they are stuck in an engagement model that prevents them from getting any better.

The good news, however, is that all of the issues are rooted in one thing: roles. They have nothing to do with technology.

The even better news is that non-IT business executives can act upon this. By changing the distribution of roles, the accompanying set of accountabilities and the measures of performance, executives can induce a profound and lasting movement to the next phase in corporate IT maturity.

You can change the center of mass, allowing technically-savvy execs and managers to take care of the processes and details required to get to the next level. Don't change the players, change the game. Don't engage yourself in the details, change the engagement model.

In volume two, we will delve into the options available to structurally change how corporate IT delivers the solutions that your business needs. The next tome is not a prognosticative thesis on what will happen in the next decade. It is rather an action-oriented set of opportunities to fast-forward your corporate IT into the future with maximum agility and speed in the use of information technology.

There is a range of choices to change the power model between those that conduct the business and those that deliver IT solutions to the former. It covers several areas from piggybacking on the heavy trends happening in the IT industry up to dismembering your monolithic corporate IT into lighter-weight teams that together create a healthier balance.*

It is my wish that you now pause and let what you've learned sink in. It is also my hope that it will create a new understanding of your your own corporate IT situation. In Volume 2, we will dive into the corporate IT engagement model change options available to accelerate the movement to a new game that foster higher quality output that in turn promote IT speed.

If you like what you read and found it useful,
I would be honored if you could provide a review at
Amazon.com. Incidentally, this will also help to influence
many more readers, since the number of reviews of a book is
a key factor in its visibility to potential buyers.

Should you have any comments, issues, opinions or personal
stories to share, I will be delighted to hear from you. You can
reach me via email at rm@the-new-age-of-it.org.

You can access my latest articles, subscribe to my newsletter
and see other people's comments and opinions at
www.the-new-age-of-IT.org.

Most articles and posts are also available on LinkedIn at
www.linkedin.com/in/rmbastien, along with very interesting
discussion threads.

NOTES & REFERENCES

[1]   For a more thorough explanation and an historical view of the subject, I suggest inspired readers to go through the first chapter of Peppard, J. and Ward, J. *The Strategic Management of Information Systems.* Fourth Edition. Wiley, 2016.

[2]   In 2001, 17 software developers discussed lightweight software development methods. They published the *Manifesto for Agile Software Development*, publicly available at http://agilemanifesto.org/. There are many good reference books on the subject, such as: Larman, Craig. *Agile and Iterative Development: A Manager's Guide.* Addison-Wesley, 2004.

[3]   Just for the sake of it, I performed an unscientific and unsystematic survey of professional blogs and magazines and came up with a list of 190 determinants of project failure[4]. You can get a list of 101 at just one site, and even a peer-reviewed taxonomy of IT-project failure[5].

[4]   Calleam Consulting. "101 Common Causes." *International Project Leadership Academy.* http://calleam.com/WTPF/?page_id=2338http://calleam.com/WTPF/?page_id=2338 Accessed: December 2017.

[5]   Al-Ahmad, Walid et al. "A Taxonomy of an IT Project Failure: Root Causes." *International Management Review. Vol. 5, No. 1, 2009.*

[6]   Denker, Ahmet. "The Challenges of Large-Scale IT Projects." *International Science Index, Industrial and Manufacturing Engineering.* Vol. 1, No. 9, 2007.

[7]   The growth of complexity and the relative costs of integration in business IT projects have been frequently denounced in the last fifteen years[8][9][10], to a point where it has almost become publicly acknowledged. But the issue hasn't gone away.

[8]   Yager, Tom. "The Future of Application Integration." *InfoWorld*. February 25, 2002.

[9]   Lheureux, Benoit et al. "Predicts 2013: Application Integration." November 14, 2012.
        Reported in: Chandrasekhar, Dinesh. "Gartner Predictions 2013 for Application Integration: My Take." *Beyond B2B*. November 26, 2012. http://www.b2b.com/blog/reality_check/index.php/integration-insights/gartner-predictions-2013-for-application-integration-my-take/
        Accessed: April 2017.

[10]   Duggan, Jim, and Sribar, Valentin. *What is the Penalty for Complexity in Application Portfolios?* Gartner, 2010.

[11]   Alexander, Christopher. *Notes on the Synthesis of Form.* Harvard University Press, 1964.

[12]   Alexander, Christopher. *The Timeless Way of Building.* Oxford University Press, 1979.

[13]   Simon, Herbert A. *The Sciences of the Artificial.* MIT Press, 1996, Chapter 5.

[14]   Depending on where you live, there are plenty of contract templates available. Some examples can be found at:
        http://www.ibanet.org for the UK, http://www.ccdc.org for Canada or https://www.aiacontracts.org in the U.S.

[15]   Such as https://www.aia.org/pages/3296-code-of-ethics—professional-conduct in the US, or
        http://legisquebec.gouv.qc.ca/en/ShowDoc/cr/A-21,%20r.%205.1 in Quebec, or http://www.legislation.govt.nz/regulation/public/2006/0161/latest/DLM388426.html for New Zealand.

[16]   Building houses, temples or bridges, however remote from IT technically speaking, is not that far-off from a who's who angle. Civil architecture itself is as old as the settlement of human nomads, but the role of the architect, as we conceive it in the Western world, dates back to a few centuries. Before that, crafts-men were also responsible for the design[18]. The definition of a balanced engagement model in the civil construction world did not come naturally, as we can guess by reading this citation from Philibert Delorme (1514-1570), a French architect and thought leader of the Renaissance:

"Patrons should employ architects instead of turning to some master mason or master carpenter as is the custom or some painter, some notary or some other person who is supposed to be qualified but often than not has no better judgment than the patron himself [...]"[19].

This quote shows that 500 years ago, the building construction industry was having its struggles, at least from a roles perspective.

[17]   Peter Weill & Jeanne W. Ross, *IT Savvy: What Top Executives Must Know to Go from Pain to Gain,* HBR Press, 2009.

[18]   Arnold Pacey, *Medieval Architecture Drawings,* Stroud: Tempus, 2007.

[19]   Catherine Wilson, "The New Professionalism in the Renais-sance," in *The Architect: Chapters in the History of the Profession,* University of California Press, 1977, page 125.

[20]   J. Ross, I. Sebastian, C. Beath, S. Scantlebury, M. Mocker, N.Fonstad, M.Kagan, K. Moloney, *Designing digital organizations,* MIT Sloan Center for Information Systems Reseach, CISR WP No. 406. March 2016.

[21]   F.P. Brooks Jr., *The Mythical Man-month: Essays on Software Engineering,* Addison-Wesley, 1975. The author expressly asked to refer to the 1995 anniversary edition (ISBN 0-201-83595-9) containing additional chapters which are as an absolute must as the rest of book.

[22] Minda Zetlin, Surviving CIO Regime Change, Computerworld, March , 2011, refers to The Society for Information Management survey of CIOs, CTOs and senior IT executives at more than 400 U.S., European, Asian and Latin American companies, October 2010. In comparison, CEOs tenure looks much longer[47], confirming a higher turnaround for CIOs.

[23] For a deeper dive into the aberration of the measurement of speed (or its lack of) in corporate IT, take a look at this short article: http://the-new-age-of-it.org/corporate-it-the-non-speed-formula/.

[24] The reader may want to browse through the report of a working group from The Royal Academy of Engineering and The British Computer Society, *The Challenges of Complex IT Projects*, 2004, on pages 13-14, where flexibility and invisibility are described as additional challenges to IT projects. Last accessed in December 2017 at: http://www.bcs.org/upload/pdf/complexity.pdf.

[25] The term silo in today's organizations takes its roots in: AME Study Group on Functional Organization, "Organizational Renewal — Tearing Down the Functional Silos," Target, Summer 1988, pp 4-14.

[26] The Project Management Institute (PMI)[27] publishes the Guide to the Project Management Body of Knowledge (PMBOK)[43] which gathers a summary of the most important good or best practices in project management, including the most widely accepted definitions of roles and responsibilities in project management: managing budget, scope and schedule are the basics, but also communications, stakeholders, dependencies with other projects, risks and more. When I was in training sessions to become a certified project management professional (PMP) back in 2001, there was a running gag from the trainer, which was closer to reality than humor: "If you're not sure who's responsible for something in your project, then by default, it's you, the PM."

[27] The Project Management Institute. See http://pmi.org for more details.

[28]   Defects are not all equal when looking at them from the angle of
         the consequences. A defect that crashes a server and deprives
         500 customer-facing users of their primary tool is catastrophic.
         If it impacts one user at a time, even customer-facing, it is not
         as catastrophic, since system unavailability is applied to only
         one user, as long as the frequency is not too high. A defect that
         crashes only one, non-customer-facing back-end administra-
         tive user at a time, once in a while, is of lesser consequence. If
         a defect does not stop any process, but loses data, it is pretty
         important but it is not in the outage (crash) category. To better
         manage these important differences, IT teams have developed
         defect rating models with clear rules for assignment of a grade to
         a defect. The grade is usually called a severity level in IT jargon.
         Severity 1, or Sev One for IT people, means that you stop what
         you were doing and fix it now.

[29]   In most mature organizations, there is a critical project manage-
         ment step called *baselining*, at which all the estimations of time
         and costs are deemed complete and frozen in time. The baseline
         then becomes the reference point for many project performance
         metrics. The baseline is what the project was supposed to cost
         and how long it was supposed to last at a certain date. The
         baseline is usually rigorously recorded. However, the baseline
         is the result of an estimation process that is mostly iterative and
         previous iteration estimates are not so rigorously recorded. Fur-
         thermore, the time at which a baseline is set and recorded varies
         from one organization to the other, and in certain cases that I
         have witnessed, the baseline is set after a significant portion of
         the budget has already been spent (10 to 50 %).

[30]   Software estimation is not new[37][38]. *Barry Boehm's book
         Software Engineering Economics* [36] dates back to 1981. There are
         several costing models such as COCOMO, COSYSMO or COCOTS
         that have been freely available for years, are well documented
         and provide dozens of already identified and tested cost drivers.

There are also fields of research devoted to measuring the functional complexity of software with estimation frameworks based on function points[34] or use case points[35].

[31] NASA, in its fourth version of its publicly available *Cost Estimation Handbook*[33], provides a wealth of methods to develop your own parametric cost estimation techniques. Other authors offer estimation techniques that take into account the whole life cycle analysis in the context of complex systems or software intensive systems[32], such as those commonly found in your corporate IT portfolio.

[32] John V. Farr, *Systems Life Cycle Costing: Economic Analysis, Estimation, and Management,* CRC Press, 2011.

[33] NASA Cost Estimating Handbook, Version 4.0, *Appendix C: Cost Estimating Methodologies,* last accessed in August 2015 at: http://www.nasa.gov/offices/ooe/CAD/nasa-cost-estimating-handbook-ceh/#.VeI5mfl_NBc.

[34] David Garmus, David Herron, *Function Point Analysis — Measurement Practices for Successful Software Projects,* Addison-Wesley, 2001.

[35] John Smith, *The Estimation of Effort Based on Use Cases,* Rational Software White Paper, Rational Software Corporation, 1999.

[36] Barry W. Boehm, *Software Engineering Economics*, Prentice-Hall PTR, 1981.

[37] A thorough review of existing techniques can be found in Ali Abbas, S. et al., "Cost Estimation: A survey of Well-known Historic Cost Estimation Techniques," *Journal of Emerging Trends in Computing and Information Sciences,* vol 3, no 4, April 2012, p. 612.

[38] There are several models that have been developed and have evolved over the years that can provide rules of thumb to IT managers, with high-level proportions of time allocated to the steps of software-related development processes. Reifer[39]

provides an overview of three models related to three different methods, where the architecture and design portions of the IT projects account for roughly 25 to 30 % of the total cost. One could rightfully argue that in software development, a portion of the construction is a form of design too, and that the actual design portion accounts for more than a quarter of the cost.

[39] Reifer, Donald, *Industry Software Cost, Quality and Productivity Benchmarks, April 2004*, last accessed Dec 2015 at: http://www.compaid.com/caiinternet/ezine/reifer-benchmarks.pdf

[40] Measures specific enough in order to answer questions such as "How much time was spent understanding what a program does before starting the 'real' work of modifying it?" or "Did you perform data mappings between two systems, and if so, which ones?", "Which component were you working on?", "When testing, were you testing functional behavior, or interfaces with other IT components not directly in-scope?", "Which architectural layer (for example user interface) were you working on?" These questions can rarely be answered in a systematic, consistent way.

[41] See http://www.opengroup.org/certifications/professional/openca for more details.

[42] Harold R. Kerzner, *Project Management Metrics, KPIs, and Dashboards: A Guide to Measuring and Monitoring Project Performance,* 2nd edition, Wiley, 2013.

[43] Project Management Institute, *A Guide to the Project Management Body of Knowledge (PMBOK® Guide)* —Fifth Edition, Project Management Institute, 2013.

[44] Project Management Professional, or PMP® is one of the certifications from the Project Management Institute[27].

[45] Certified ScrumMaster® certification by the Scrum Alliance. See https://www.scrumalliance.org/ for more details.

[46] See www.cmmiinstitute.com for more details on Carnegie Mellon University's initiative to improve organizational capabilities.

[47] Susan Adams, CEOs Staying in Their Jobs Longer, Forbes, April 2014. Last accessed October 2015 at: http://www.forbes.com/sites/susanadams/2014/04/11/ceos-staying-in-their-jobs-longer/

[48] ITIL® started in the 80's as a British governmental initiative. More details on ITIL can be found at the official web site at https://www.axelos.com/best-practice-solutions/itil/what-is-itil.

[49] The Standish Group has been publishing a very frequently cited report since 1994 that shows the success and failure rates of IT projects: the CHAOS Report[51]. One of the reasons for such fame is the high failure rate and low success rate shown in these reports. In the 2013 version of the CHAOS Manifesto[52], the Standish Group presents successful projects' rates going up from 29% to 39% between 2002 and 2012, and failure rates ranging between 18% and 24% during that period. Despite a positive trend over the past ten years, and some observers finding these reports unfairly skewed toward failure[53], such figures should nevertheless trigger genuine concern. The CHAOS report is not the only source of concern. A study[50] from McKinsey & Company and Oxford University showed that on average, large IT projects ran 45% over budget and 7% over schedule, while delivering 56% less value than planned.

[50] Michael Bloch, Sven Blumberg, Jürgen Laartz, *Delivering Large-scale IT Projects on Time, on Budget and on Value,* Insight & Publications, McKinsey & Company, October 2012. Last retrieved in August 2015 at: http://www.mckinsey.com/insights/business_technology/delivering_large-scale_it_projects_on_time_on_budget_and_on_value.

[51] The latest CHAOS report can be found at: https://www.standishgroup.com/store/https://www.standishgroup.com/store/

[52]   The Standish Group International, Inc., CHAOS Manifesto 2013. Last accessed in August 2015 at: https://larlet.fr/static/david/ stream/ChaosManifesto2013.pdf.

[53]   J. Laurez Eveleens, Chris Verhoef, *The Rise and Fall of the Chaos Report Figures,* IEEE Software, January/February 2010, p. 30-36.

[54]   Accenture, Executives Report that Mergers and Acquisitions Fail to Create Adequate Value, June 14, 2006, last accessed January 2016 at: https://newsroom.accenture.com/news/executives-report-that-mergers-and-acquisitions-fail-to-create-adequate-value.htm